Wrestling
with the Text

Wrestling with the Text

Young Adult Perspectives on Scripture

Edited by
Keith Graber Miller
Malinda Elizabeth Berry
Foreword by Mary H. Schertz

Journeys with
Scripture Series
Volume 2

Cascadia
Publishing House
Telford, Pennsylvania

copublished with
Herald Press
Scottdale, Pennsylvania

Cascadia Publishing House orders, information, reprint permissions:
contact@CascadiaPublishingHouse.com
1-215-723-9125
126 Klingerman Road, Telford PA 18969
www.CascadiaPublishingHouse.com

Wrestling with the Text
Copyright © 2007 by Cascadia Publishing House,
Telford, PA 18969

Copublished with Herald Press, Scottdale, PA
Library of Congress Catalog Number: 2006036870
ISBN 13: 978-1-931038-37-9; **ISBN 10:** 1-931038-37-6
Printed in the United States of America
Book design by Cascadia Publishing House
Cover design by Merrill R. Miller

The paper used in this publication is recycled and meets the
minimum requirements of American National Standard for Information Sci-
ences—Permanence of Paper for Printed Library Materials, ANSI Z39.48-1984.
All Bible quotations are used by permission, all rights reserved and unless otherwise
noted are from *The New Revised Standard Version of the Bible*, copyright 1989, by
the Division of Christian Education of the National Council of the Churches of
Christ in the USA. Quotes marked NIV are from *The Holy Bible, New International
Version*, copyright © 1973, 1978, 1984 International Bible Society, Zondervan Bible
Publishers; KJV from the King James Version of the Bible.

Library of Congress Cataloguing-in-Publication Data
Wrestling with the text : young adult perspectives on scripture / edited by Keith
Graber Miller and Malinda Elizabeth Berry.
    p. cm.
Includes bibliographical references and index.
ISBN-13: 978-1-931038-37-9 (6 x 9" trade pbk. : alk. paper)
ISBN-10: 1-931038-37-6 (6 x 9" trade pbk. : alk. paper)
1. Young adults--Religious life. 2. Bible--Criticism, interpretation, etc. 3. Men-
nonite Church--Doctrines. I. Graber Miller, Keith, 1959- II. Berry, Malinda Eliza-
beth, 1974- III. Title.

BV4529.2.W74 2007
220.084'2--dc22

                                                                    2006036870

        14 13 12 11 10 09 08 07   10 9 8 7 6 5 4 3 2 1

To Simon, Mia, and Niles,
for whom I hope the text always has meaning
—KGM

To the Habeggerians:
Our living room was a great wrestling ring,
wasn't it?
—MEB

Contents

Foreword

A good book of essays will work both as individual pieces and as a whole. *Wrestling with the Text* is such a book. Each of the stories in this collection is interesting on its own terms. The essays together, however, transcend the disparate voices to provide a partial, but fascinating and multi-layered, answer to the question of how Scripture forms us as the people of God.

As a Scripture teacher, I have participated in the laments that Keith Graber Miller references in the introduction. I have had many conversations with students, church people, and colleagues that touch on an anxiety that we are losing our sense of the biblical text. We fear that we are losing the use of the Bible as a resource for faithful living. We talk about biblical illiteracy and wonder about an eroding dedication to discover the Living Word within the Word.

What these stories reveal is that we are not losing our sense of the text even as our sense of how we relate to the text is changing. Change is, of course, the birthright of every new generation. If a tradition is to remain vital, it must be owned and owned anew, owned in unconventional and sometimes disconcerting ways, by those who carry the tradition forward. I encourage readers to read these essays with an openness to how the Spirit is moving in the interaction of these young adults with the biblical text. If Scripture is, as I believe, like music that must be performed to be known and understood,[1] then these young people are performing with their hearts as well as their minds. These stories are honest and courageous; they have much to teach us.

Let me suggest two ways I think the Spirit is moving through the pages of this book. One is an emerging view of the authority of Scripture, a concept that we have likely used badly as often as we have used it well. Biblical scholar Ellen F. Davis has suggested that we might think about teaching the Bible *confessionally*. To read confessionally, to put Scripture at the "functional center" of our lives as believers is to orient our conversations, our programs and our discernment to the challenges and comforts of Scripture. "Reading the Bible confessionally," she says

> means recognizing it as a word that is indispensable if we are to view the world realistically and hopefully. We acknowledge it as a divine word that is uniquely powerful to interpret our experience. But more, we allow ourselves to be moved by it, trusting that it is the one reliable guide to a life that is not, in the last analysis, desperate.[2]

The young adults writing in this book, I believe, help us move toward that healthier and livelier concept of the authority of Scripture.

A second way I think the Spirit is moving through the pages of this book is the window the stories give us into how a scriptural tradition is carried from one generation to the next. In the response section of the book, Nancy Tatom Ammerman makes the important observation that if the biblical canon matters to the church, it is essential that we build a core of experience and meaning around these texts that we have agreed to share. She also observes that the faith tradition from which and in which these young adults find their voices has not only told them the biblical stories that fund their imaginations but has given them space and opportunity to raise questions about the text and to debate the text. Ammerman is right, I think, but as an insider I would never have been able to identify and celebrate the gift so clearly.

This is a generous book. The younger writers are generous with their experience; the older commentators are generous with their nurture of that experience. It is a book that gives me heart for the rest of my journey as a Scripture teacher in the church.

—*Mary H. Schertz, Elkhart, Indiana*
  Professor of New Testament, Associated Mennonite Biblical Seminary

Notes

1. In *The Art of Reading Scripture,* ed. Ellen F. Davis and Richard B. Hays (Grand Rapids: Eerdmans, 2003), 3.

2. Ibid., 9-10.

Introduction

Keith Graber Miller and Malinda Elizabeth Berry

Nearly a decade ago, in a plane bound for Albuquerque, I (Keith) found myself browsing through the January issue of *American Way* magazine, the airline's promotional publication. There I came across an interview with Robertson Davies, Canada's "champion of letters," widely recognized before his death as Canada's greatest writer. After speaking about everything from David Letterman to whether there is a kind of evangelical mission in his writing to his non-use of computers, Davies turned his attention to the Bible.

In earlier speeches Davies had mourned the loss of the Bible not only as a religious guide but also as a shared source of literature for our culture. When asked about this by the *American Way* interviewer, Davies said,

> Well, it's a source of reference, you see, and it's a very great thing in any culture to have some classical literature to which you can refer with the confidence that most of the people you're talking to share it and know what's in it. That used to be the case with the Bible because it is classical literature . . . which everybody used to know. But they *don't* know it anymore and that means that a big frame of reference has been lost.[1]

Moments after reading the interview with Davies, I was off the plane and at the Society of Christian Ethics' annual conference. Ironically, the first session I attended that day included a paper by John P. Burgess titled "Does Scripture Matter? Scripture as Ethical Norm in a Time of Ecclesial Crisis." The paper began with a reference to Ezra and

Nehemiah's accounts of the return of the Hebrew exiles to Judah. The story is familiar to many: Jerusalem had fallen to the Babylonians in 587 BCE, and half a century later, the Babylonian king Cyrus had allowed some of the exiles to return and attempt to rebuild the temple and the walls of Jerusalem. When Ezra summoned the people to hear the words of the law of Moses, they gathered together before the Water Gate. He and others read from it from early morning until midday, and the ears of all the people were attentive to the book of the law. And as the readers spoke the holy words from the book, all the people *wept* as they recognized their own fallibility and God's grace (Neh. 8:9, emph. added).[2]

Beginning a paper at an academic conference with this story was extraordinarily moving and adeptly led the listener into the author's argument that Scripture does *indeed* matter. It has compelling power and continues to be the source of the church's life.

What was striking to me were the common themes in the lamentations of these two quite distinct voices—ones I heard over the course of a few hours. The novelist and the ethicist, for different reasons, both were disturbed by what appeared to them the diminishment of biblical knowledge and biblical authority in the North American context. Both were calling, either implicitly or explicitly, for a rediscovery of the text, encounters with the written Word that have decisively influenced multiple individuals, communities, and cultures that have come before us.

Journeys with Scripture

This text began germinating several years ago when we began wondering whether among young adults in the United States biblical knowledge and appreciation for biblical authority have, in fact, diminished. I (Malinda) am in the Generation X cohort, the group whose perspectives on Scripture we were seeking to ascertain, and I have had a chance to teach both at the college and seminary level, interacting with many other students my age and younger. As a professor of religion, I (Keith) regularly have contacts with reflective students and graduates, including Malinda and some of the others who shared their perspectives with us in this volume. As Mennonites educated in and teaching at a Mennonite institution, we were particularly interested in whether Davies' charge was true for those raised in or presently committed to the Anabaptist-Mennonite tradition, which for us has historically been steeped in Scripture.

Some of our suspicions—particularly about the biblical knowledge of young adults—were ill-founded, at least among the contributors to this volume, who probably are not fully representative of young people within even one denominational stream. Many of the authors make reference to family or personal devotional times that included Bible reading. About half participated in some sort of Bible memorization program, either self-initiated or through their local congregation. That is not to say that all the writers included here know their Bibles well; some do not get all the "facts" of biblical canonical history "correct"; some offer insights that would not hold water with conventional wisdom in biblical studies circles. The authors are not necessarily—or certainly not *all*—biblical scholars, though some are in or have completed seminary and others are in graduate school.

Many contributors *do* speak of some resistance to biblical authority or ignore the topic of authority altogether. In our discussions with the young adults whose stories are included here, some noted that the language of "authority" does not resonate with them and does not represent how they think about the biblical text. Others spoke about the growing skepticism toward political authority in the United States, a skepticism that began in the 1960s with resistance to the Vietnam War, deepened with the 1970s and Watergate and the Reagan years, and were further challenged by the Clinton sex scandals and the George W. Bush administration's apparent lies or exaggerations about the imminent threat Iraq posed to the world after September 11, 2001.

Certainly, when set within a larger postmodern context like ours that challenges traditional authority, *any* text, leadership group, or entity that claims authority has its work cut out for it. Even though postmodernism, at its best, values community, the life stage of most young adults is still one of autonomy. That desire for autonomy may run against the grain of historic Anabaptist-Mennonite commitments to community and *Gelassenheit* (yieldedness).

Contributors to this volume also noted that today they are inundated with information—signs and texts and marketing ploys and electronic messages that call for their attention. They also are aware of what one describes as "the mythology of *sola scriptura*," the Reformation notion that faith and life are guided by "Scripture alone." Most—subconsciously if not consciously—believe what I (Malinda) refer to in my chapter as the Methodist Quadrilateral: the reality that Scripture (sacred texts), the faith tradition, reason, and personal experience all inform our faith and our ethics. Several of the authors refer to feminist theology's impact on their understandings of Scripture, both for feminism's critique of patriarchal and oppressive structures and texts and for its valuing of women's experience. Other liberationist perspectives that have emerged since the 1960s also have emphasized experience as a lens through which to view Scripture, reason, and tradition in ways that resonate with this generation of Mennonite young adults committed to the relatively recent social justice concerns of Mennonites.

For young adults today, then, considering the biblical text authoritative is an *active choice*; that contrasts dramatically with the experience of most middle-age and older people, at least among Mennonites, who, in their early years, perceived the Bible as a *given*, the authority out of which they were living. The notion of *choice* regarding one's embrace or dismissal of biblical authority makes the experience of young adults—even those within a voluntary, believers' baptism tradition—different from that of their elders. Those contributors who continue to acknowledge the authority of the Bible speak about *giving* the text authority rather than believing it inherently *has* authority.

As we know from college classroom experience, many students arrive on campus convinced that—whatever the Bible might say—it can clearly say anything we want it to. Or so it has seemed from what they have observed in church fights during their young lives. In a paper one student wrote for a course at a Mennonite college, she observed, "The Bible has become a place where warring factions go for ammunition." Most teenagers and young adults have seen the biblical text aggressively launched over issues related to homosexual practice. Earlier, some of us cut our biblical teeth on arguments about divorce or women in leadership.

For me (Keith), the issue was headcoverings. As a child growing up in a faithful Mennonite congregation, my first cognitive encounter with the biblical text as a source of authority was in 1970, when my two slightly older sisters joined their peers in refusing to wear the traditional Mennonite headcovering upon their baptism into the church. I was eleven then, awestruck by the bravery of my sisters.

After congregational leaders preached sermons, discussed the issue at church council, and debated what the Bible said about women covering their heads, they determined that young women would be *encour-*

aged to wear the headcovering but that it would not be *obligatory*. Slowly, incrementally, the headcoverings vanished, not only from the seventh- and eighth-graders' heads, but then from those in their later teens, then the twenty-somethings, then the mothers of the adolescent girls. Then only a few white nets remained, perched on the heads of the very oldest congregational members. Indelibly etched in my pre-pubescent mind was the recognition of the interpretive possibilities posed by the biblical text, the way in which the Bible was a humanly constructed and sometimes deconstructed authority.

In an all-or-nothing context—and that is how many issues and debates are constructed—change inevitably undermines that which has come before. But it need not be all or nothing; there are alternatives. As Stanley Hauerwas has written, "Traditions by their nature require change, since there can be no tradition without interpretation. And interpretation is the constant adjustment that is required if the current community is to stay in continuity with tradition."[3] Hauerwas approvingly quotes J. P. Mackey's remark in *Tradition and Change in the Church*[4] that "Tradition means continuity and change, both together and both equally."[5]

We remember how grateful we were for Hauerwas's rendering of the nature of biblical authority when we first came across it in *A Community of Character*. Hauerwas writes,

> By regarding Scripture as an authority Christians mean to indicate that they find there the traditions through which their community most nearly comes to knowing and being faithful to the truth. Scripture is not meant to be a problem solver. It rather describes the process whereby the community we call the church is initiated by certain texts into what Barr has called the "vivid and lively pattern of argument and controversy" characteristic of biblical traditions.[6]

To claim Scripture as authority, then, is not claiming that it is errorless, or that its genres or understandings are unique, or that its images are essential for us to know who we are. Again, we find Hauerwas helpful when he says,

> Rather, to claim the Bible as authority is the testimony of the church that this book provides the resources necessary for the church to be a community sufficiently truthful so that our con-

versation with one another and God can continue across generations. . . . By trying to live, think, and feel faithful to its witness
[we] find [we] are more nearly able to live faithful to the truth.[7]

Telling Our Stories

Not all of the contributors to this volume are convinced that the
Bible provides the resources necessary for a sufficiently truthful community. Some essays make arguments we think are compelling; we disagree
sharply with others. Some make us, as teachers of impressionable young
people, even more conscious—if not terrified—of the power of the
classroom. Some responses sadden us, and others bring us immense joy.
Nearly all of the writers make some reference to "wrestling" or "struggling" with Scripture, and for that we are deeply grateful. At some level,
Scripture does matter to the young adults represented here, as is evi-
denced by their willingness to write on this topic and show up for a
weekend to discuss their journeys.

All of the essays in Part One emerged out of a Journeys with Scripture colloquy we helped host in New York City in June 2003. The colloquy was the second such event in a thirteenth-month period, following
on the heels of a similar gathering the previous year at Laurelville Mennonite Church Center in western Pennsylvania.[8]

Several tensions in the church and in American culture gave rise to
that initial Scripture colloquy, which included two dozen professors,
church administrators, and other present and potential church leaders.
As pacifist Christians and members of a denomination in the Historic
Peace Church tradition, we were troubled by the events surrounding
September 11, 2001. And, like so many other Christian denominations in the United States, Mennonites have been struggling to understand the role Scripture's authority plays in our discussions of homosexuality.

This was the context in which we told our stories at that first colloquy, looking for common ground and wondering how to build bridges
to traverse the gaps created by our differences. We took our cues from
Walter Brueggemann, who has observed that attentiveness to the ways
we have come to know the Bible "may lead us to recognize that the story
of someone else's nurture in the faith could be a transformative gift that
allows us to read the text in a new way."[9] By framing our weekend as one

of storytelling, we were engaging a theological method that follows the patterns of narrative theology.

As a method, narrative theology gives us a way to situate our faith stories as well as providing an anchor as we begin the process of evaluating what makes a story worth telling whether it is the first telling or the hundredth. In his survey of Christian theology, Alister McGrath outlines narrative theology as thinking that is based on the observation that the Bible tells us stories about God.[10] In Hebrew Scriptures, we have tales of God's faithfulness to God's people Israel. Christian Scriptures, then, relate stories that characterize God as our redeemer through Jesus Christ.

From McGrath's perspective, the appeal of a narrative approach to reading the Bible is four-fold. First, narrative is the main literary form in Scripture; as we affirm our faith in Jesus Christ, we also affirm the patterns of narrative that convey God's story to us. Second, rather than analyzing cold, hard facts, narrative theology invites us to use our imaginations and reflect on the images of a story. Third, narrative theology affirms that God meets us in history. Our stories and God's story intersect at points that have an impact on our ethical understandings. These intersections change our ethical viewpoints but do not necessarily define them. "The gospel is not primarily about a set of ethical principles; it is about the effect of an encounter with God upon the lives of individuals and the histories of nations."[11] Fourth, when we observe and affirm the narrative quality of the biblical text, we begin to see the tension between our limited knowledge as human beings on the one hand and God's omniscience on the other.

For the June 2003 Journeys with Scripture colloquy, we employed this same narrative format, allowing all twenty-eight participants to tell part of their own journey with the biblical text. Twelve participants at the colloquy were women; sixteen were men. Six of the colloquy participants were people of color; eight were not raised in Mennonite homes but had later affiliated with Mennonites; and at least six were or had been pastors. Eight were present or retired faculty members at Mennonite colleges or universities, and four others worked for church institutions. Five were in some sort of voluntary service at the time of the colloquy, and seven others were in or preparing for graduate school.

Some of the participants *over* thirty years old[12] (affectionately referred to at the colloquy as "older than Jesus") tell their stories in another

Cascadia/Herald Press text.[13] In New York, these older participants were asked to briefly report on a transformative moment in their lives with the Bible. Participants *under* thirty years old—those "younger than Jesus"—were asked to provide a fuller narrative, identifying initial impressions of Scripture, perspectives on the authority of Scripture, critical turning points in their understandings or commitments, and ways in which Scripture does or does not form their Mennonite/religious identity. All sixteen of those accounts are included here.

During the four days we met together at Union Theological Seminary in New York, we spoke directly and honestly about our journeys as well as the presuppositions that we bring to the biblical text. In an afternoon discussion of what we bring to the biblical text, older and younger participants acknowledged the lenses or sieves that shape their reading of the Bible, their interpretation of its words, and their acceptance of its value. Among those presuppositions was the belief in the primacy of God's love, or the conviction that God is a God of beauty, or that God is "other," or that God is *not a capricious* deity. Several said Jesus is more authoritative than the text itself, though they recognized that most of their information about Jesus comes from the Bible. Another said his conviction that God has a preferential option for the poor, a theme brought to light since the 1960s in Latin American liberation theology, shapes his reading of the text. Another said the New Testament in particular is about justice: "Repent, for the reign of God is at hand," and this is "not Mennonite peace or nonresistance, but justice." One participant said he operates with the belief that the world is moving forward, that there is some kind of beginning and an end.

Presuppositions regarding the text itself included the recognition that the Bible is an ancient book, one written long ago by writers who had their own presuppositions. A narrative holds the Bible together, said one participant, while another added that the text should not be harmonized; harmonizing it is doing violence to it. Another raised the possibility that there is no ultimate cohesion in the Bible, and asked what that would mean for the community of believers. One participant wondered aloud whether the Bible would have been different had it been written by women. Several acknowledged that the Bible is not a flat text, dropped from heaven, with all chapters and verses equally instructive for faithful living today. Some participants noted that the Bible is always contingent, and that it speaks to us only indirectly, not directly. Another, in response, said that the Bible is "God's living word to *me*: it has something to say to *me*," and another said, "The biblical text is revealed by God." Two said they presuppose that Christians who read the Bible will do something with what they read, and that they constantly ask what new things God is trying to do with our faith communities.

Some young adults at the colloquy admitted they were surprised to be invited, given that they are still asking themselves, "Who will be my community for life? Who are my people?" Most participants said being asked to write their stories provided them with the opportunity to think more carefully about how they approach the Bible. Some said it was powerful to think of themselves as being "captured" by Scripture; others were inspired to take the Scripture seriously; others said in the future they will seek to be more hospitable to Scripture. Among the older adult participants, some noted their appreciation for the candor and trust evident at the gathering. Some admitted they were initially shocked by the lack of reverence some participants had for Scripture, though they also saw them as on a dynamic journey, grappling with the role of the Bible in their lives and sorting out their place in the church. After hearing the stories, one "older than Jesus" participant remarked, "The church has a future!" Some wondered where in the church it is safe to tell these stories, and how such dialogue can be fostered.

Among the purposes for the New York gathering, as we expressed at the beginning of our time together, were these:

- to encourage young adults in their journey with Scripture and with their religious identity;
- to provide a space for fellowship between young adults in their twenties and between young adults and their older peers, including, in some cases, several of their former professors;
- to allow professors and other church leaders to gain a better understanding of young adults' journeys with Scripture and related sense of religious identity;
- to explore how the Bible functions for young and older people today. Does it continue to have an identity-framing role, as it did for many Christians, or at least Anabaptist-Mennonites, in earlier generations? What watersheds might have occurred in the last several decades? If not the Bible, what forces are presently shaping religious identity for young adults in or along the margins of the church?

In a background paper for the first Journeys with Scripture collo-quy, Ray Gingerich and Earl Zimmerman wrote that

> The Scriptures, we believe, are a significant and abiding phenom-enon in our Christian and Anabaptist heritage. Our understand-ings of Scripture lie beneath the current discussions on both non-violence and homosexuality (and other issues) and will play a vital role in how we as a church continue to struggle with these is-sues. In floating this concept among colleagues and friends, we received unanimous affirmation that the Scriptures belong to the Anabaptist-Mennonite matrix that shapes our ethical under-standings and identity—and consequently, how we practice our faith. Our understandings of Scripture will impact all other major issues the church will face in this new era. We believe that as a church we are long overdue an open and confessional conver-sation, sharing our struggles with the Scriptures and our commit-ment to them.

Struggling with the Bible

As we already noted above, the idea of "struggling" with Scripture is a repeated refrain in the essays in Part One; as such, it becomes a key theme within this volume. We are reminded of the image of Jacob's wrestling with God's messenger all night at the Jabbok river (Gen. 32:22-32). Some contributors here have wrestled until they have re-ceived their blessing; for some, that blessing has come with a biblical limp. The role of historical criticism of the Bible is a given for most of the contributors. In contrast to those a generation or two older, these young adults' skepticism about the text has less to do with methods of analysis and interpretation (though those issues still emerge) and more to do with reverencing the text as special or unique. In a similar vein, as we noted, was the lack of resonance many of our contributors feel for the language of "authority."

Our general sense is that Mennonite high schools, colleges, and seminaries thoughtfully help students wrestle with their faith and with Scripture during those formative years, pushing them to examine and analyze and—at their best, re-embrace—Scripture. Those Mennonite young adults who attend other colleges and universities often begin that struggle later. We make these admittedly unverifiable assertions based not only on the contributors here, most of whom attended Mennonite educational institutions, but on our larger interactions with Mennonite and other Christian students in places where we have taught.

However, we are keenly conscious of the fact that, long before now, gone were the days (if they ever existed) that erudite, urbane Mennonite college professors needed to dismantle their charges' rural, naïve embrace of a flat text. Many or most students now go to college with only minimal biblical knowledge, unless they have been to a parochial secondary school. Most do not even *know* the biblical narrative well enough to *reject* it. As these essays make clear, that leaves college and seminary professors with a tremendous amount of power over students' lives, faith, and valuing of Scripture. As teachers, we find that power, and the responsibility that comes with it, both frightening and challenging. We want our students to critically examine Christian faith and the text that illuminates it, but we also want them to choose to continue living within this dynamic tradition of biblical faith.

Another common theme we discovered in these essays also was referred to above: the primacy for many, though not all of the writers, of personal experience as a source for guiding faith and life. This source of experience, in many cases, trumps the Bible or any other text or tradition. In his essay, Kevin Maness says that his "faith, belief, and identity are built on a multifaceted foundation, consisting of my experience (both personal and indirect), my intellectual meanderings, the people in my life, and the texts that I have experienced, including the Bible, other religious texts, and the wider world of literature." A handful of writers speak about the way in which feminist theologians (particularly Rosemary Radford Ruether and Elisabeth Schüssler Fiorenza) influenced their response to the Bible, allowing them to critique the biblical text in a new way *and* to value their own experiences of God and the world. Although the language differs from writer to writer, many refer to some efforts at reconceptualizing Scripture and their relationship to the text.

In the essays, many contributors also point to the church's use and abuse of the Bible, making frequent reference to how the text has been used against women and against gay and lesbian people. In describing his experience in one college course, Daniel Shank Cruz says he realized that "institutional Christianity was really oppressive to a lot of women, including some of my closest friends. Midway through the class I came to believe that I could no longer associate with the Christian church because of its oppressiveness, which was in sharp contrast to Jesus' liberating teachings."

A related theme in the essays is justice, as it relates to gender and race in the church and in our culture. Some contributors see the church as failing miserably in the areas of justice within its ranks, or of not seeking justice sufficiently in the church and world. At the colloquy, when I (Keith) quoted the old adage, "The church is a treasure, but a treasure in earthen vessels, carried forward by fallible people like you and like me"—a challenge my students often hear—one "younger than Jesus" participant said, "The humanness of the church is not all that appealing."

As many writers note, flannelgraph retellings of biblical stories and illustrated children's Bibles etched themselves into their hearts and minds, though some feel ambivalent about those (usually white, Western-looking) images. Additionally, the Bible quizzing, regular memorization, and routine family devotions that are part of many of these stories demonstrate that the text was bred into their bones in ways that have indelibly shaped their characters, formed them in ways they cannot shake, even if they were to now leave the Bible behind. We sense, though, that these ways of being embedded in Scripture are, by now, found only in small pockets of the Mennonite church and perhaps most other churches in the United States. Given the trajectory we perceive, it is difficult to imagine—though we wish it were not so—that future generations will have even the elementary level of biblical literacy that comes from regularly hearing and memorizing texts in their homes, a significant supplement to weekly reading of the Bible from the pulpit.

With Gratitude. . . .

Given the vulnerability necessitated in telling our stories of faith, we are exceedingly grateful for the spirited cooperation of the contributors to this volume. We suspect their journeys will resonate with many others of their generation, and we are certain their narratives will inform pastors, professors, and other lay leaders for years to come. Thanks also go to our thoughtful respondents, Nancy Tatom Ammerman, Pam Dintaman, and Valerie Weaver-Zercher, who write from their perspectives as a sociologist, pastor, and writer/editor, respectively. Michael A. King, publisher at Cascadia Publishing House, has been a delightful and supportive guide and friend throughout this process.

We also are grateful to the many people who assisted with the New York colloquy. Alicia Miller and Daniel Shank Cruz, both of whom were Mennonite Voluntary Service workers in New York at the time, helped with a wide range of logistical details at the colloquy—securing meeting locations, arranging housing, and scheduling meals and entertainment. Krista Dutt and Robert Rhodes worked with me (Malinda) to plan worship experiences at the colloquy, including the reading in Appendix A in this text and a sermon by Robert.

J. Denny Weaver, Ray Gingerich, Earl Zimmerman, John Kampen, and Paul Keim, all veterans of the first Journeys with Scripture colloquy, provided wise counsel in the months before our New York sojourn. Thanks also to Nicole Olivia Cober Bauman, our extraordinary assistant, who carefully read through the proofs and completed the tedious task of drafting the Subject and Scripture Indexes.

We dedicate this volume to our past, present and future students with the words of Paul to the church at Rome:

> Now to God who is able to strengthen you according to my gospel and the proclamation of Jesus Christ, according to the revelation of the mystery that was kept secret for long ages but is now disclosed, and through the prophetic writings is made known to all the Gentiles, according to the command of the eternal God, to bring about the obedience of faith—to the only wise God, through Jesus Christ, to whom be the glory forever! Amen. (Rom. 16:25-27)

We wish you, and all the readers of this text, honest critiquing, clear visioning, and faithful seeking on your journeys with Scripture.

Notes

1. Chuck Thompson, "Canada's Champion of Letters," *American Way* (Jan. 1. 1996): 97.

2. All Scripture passages cited here are from New Revised Standard Version.

3. Stanley Hauerwas, *A Community of Character* (Notre Dame: University of Notre Dame Press, 1991): 61.

4. J. P. Mackey, *Tradition and Change in the Church* (Dayton: Pflaum Press, 1968): 42-43.

5. Hauerwas, loc.cit., 61.

6. Ibid., 63.

7. Ibid., 63-64.

8. Ray Gingerich and Earl Zimmerman of Eastern Mennonite University were the primary planners of the first Journeys with Scripture colloquy, with consultation from J. Denny Weaver and John Kampen of Bluffton College; Paul Keim of Goshen College; and Malinda and Keith. Keith also secured a small institutional grant from the Rhodes Consultation for the Future of the Church-Related College, which helped pay some of the travel and lodging expenses for both colloquies.

9. Walter Brueggemann, "Biblical Authority: A Personal Reflection," *Christian Century* (Jan. 3-10, 2001): 14.

10. Alister McGrath, *Christian Theology: An Introduction* (Oxford: Blackwell, 2001): 167-170.

11. Ibid., 173.

12. Included among the over-thirty presenters were Addie Banks, Michael Banks, Ray Gingerich, Keith Graber Miller, John Kampen, Paul Keim, Robert Rhodes, Steve Ropp, Regina Shands Stoltzfus, J. Denny Weaver, Gary Yamasaki, and Earl Zimmerman.

13. Ray Gingerich and Earl Zimmerman, eds., *Telling Our Stories: Personal Accounts of Engagements with Scripture* (Telford, Pa.: Cascadia Publishing House, 2006).

Part One

Journeys with Scripture

CHAPTER 1

Incorporating
the Scriptures Bodily

Yvonne C. Zimmerman

For as long as I can remember, in my grandparents' dining room has hung a painting that depicts the scene from Luke 24 of Jesus and the disciples walking along the road to Emmaus. The figures in the painting are walking down a dirt road through a dense green forest. They have just crossed a wooden bridge that fords a small stream; the buildings of a town—presumably Emmaus—stand on a hill that is situated just on the other side of the forest. The scene is suspiciously similar to the way I have always imagined the Celestial City from *Little Pilgrim's Progress* would look from a distance.

"I Have Called You Friends. . . . "

I am one of those "cradle" Christians. Even before I could talk, I was socialized into the Christian world: Bible stories, bedtime prayers, Scripture songs, and Sunday school—the whole works. I grew up in Lancaster County, Pennsylvania, and in the common practice of the Mennonite churches in Lancaster during that time, I was encouraged to "make a decision for Christ"—that is, accept Jesus as my personal Lord and Savior—at an early age. And so, as I like to recount now, I "left my life of sin" at the age of nine. Whether there was much sin in my life of which my nine-year-old self could take leave, when I look back on how I "got saved" I do not so much recall what I left behind as I am aware of what I *embraced.*

Even though I grew up in a very devout family, we did not have family devotions. Be that as it may, somewhere along the way I picked up that becoming a Christian, as I did in February 1986, meant that I should begin having devotions on my own. Perhaps this was a distillation of a lifetime, however short, of warnings against the vices of being merely a "Sunday" Christian.

So I commenced daily Bible reading. To guide my reading, I used the devotional series titled *Keys for Kids* distributed through the Children's Bible Hour. I listened to Uncle Charlie and the Children's Bible Hour at nine o'clock every Saturday morning on WDAC for as far back as I can remember. There were no Saturday morning cartoons for the Zimmerman girls. Around seventh grade, however, I outgrew *Keys for Kids*. Rather than using another devotional guide, I decided I would start in Genesis and read straight through the Bible.

At the same time, I decided I would begin to memorize Bible verses, one passage a week. Each week I would select a passage—not necessarily in correspondence with my week's Bible readings—and write it on an index card using my finest, scrawly adolescent-girl handwriting. I spent a few minutes each day working on memorizing the verses until, at the end of the week, I could write them out by heart.

When I had successfully mastered a passage, I would punch a hole in the upper left-hand corner of the card and add it to the binder-ring that contained all the cards of the verses I had memorized. At the start of each week, I would start the process of creating a new card with a new passage written on it all over again. I recall clearly the first verse on my ring binder of cards: Galatians 6:9. "Let us not become weary in doing good, for at the proper time we will reap a harvest if we do not give up."[1]

I do not know whether or not memorizing a weekly Bible passage qualifies per the Galatians verse as "doing good," but at any rate, I most certainly did *not* give up. I continued both to faithfully read my Bible daily and to memorize weekly Bible verses all the way through most of high school. And I have, without a doubt, definitely "reaped a harvest."

My Bible memory sometimes lacked an effort to think critically about my chosen text. Why, I now wonder, did I feel compelled to memorize 1 Timothy 1: 15: "Here is a trustworthy saying that deserves full acceptance: Christ Jesus came into the world to save sinners of whom I am the worst"? Moreover, sometimes my Bible memory selections, in retrospect, bordered on offensive: "What *other* nation is so great as to have their gods near them the way the Lord our God is near us . . . ?" (Deut. 4:7; emph. added).

At other times, my Bible memory was aesthetically beautiful: "He heals the broken hearted and binds up their wounds. He determines the numbers of the stars and calls them each by name" (Ps. 147:3-4). Still other times, the Bible memory was inspirational—invoking genuinely virtuous character:

> Is not this the kind of fasting I have chosen to loose the chains of injustice and untie the cords of the yoke, to set the oppressed free and break every yoke? Is it not to share your food with the hungry and to provide the poor wanderer with shelter—when you see the naked, to clothe [her] and not to turn away from your own flesh and blood? Then your light will break forth like the dawn, and your healing will quickly appear; then your righteousness will go before you and the glory of the Lord will be your rear guard. (Isa. 58:6-8)

Perhaps ironically, the final passage in the index cards that were my personal Bible memory program during these years was John 15:15-16:

> "I no longer call you servants, because a servant does not know his master's business. Instead, I have called you friends, for everything that I learned from my father I have made known to you. You did not choose me, but I chose you and appointed you to go and bear fruit—fruit that will last. . . ."

From Reaping a Harvest to Bearing Fruit

I was by no means the only child either reading her Bible and/or memorizing Scripture during her adolescent years. Clearly these were the kinds of activities in which we young Christians believed we were supposed to be engaging—the fruits we were supposed to be bearing. Yet it seems to me that for a twelve-year-old—or, even more, for a significant chunk of demographically similar then-twelve-year-olds who have contributed to this book—to independently initiate and sustain a regimen of Bible reading and Bible memory provides a fascinating entrée to spiritual formation and development. I will often say in jest that I took Psalm 119:11 very literally: "I have hidden your word in my heart that I might not sin against you."

A good number of years removed from engaging in this discipline, these Scriptures are still with me. They still routinely spring to mind; they move within me; they poke their heads like freshly sprouted plants in the spring. It is not, for example, uncommon for me to find myself lifting up my eyes to the hills, hiding in the shelter of the Most High, or rising on the wings of the dawn or settling on the far side of the sea during my morning runs. In other words, these Scriptures have become a significant part of my ongoing frame of reference for engaging the world.

Whether I *like* it not; whether I *believe* them or not; whether I consciously invoke them or not, these Scriptures have become part of my interaction with my own life. These are the things that most frequently pop into my mind, however (at times) uninvited, however unintentional, however random.

"Can a mother forget the baby at her breast and have no compassion on the child she has borne? Though she may forget, I will not forget. . . . See, I have engraved you on the palms of my hands" (Isa. 49:15-16).

Engraved on the palms of my hands.

Hidden in my heart.

Inscribed on my forehead.

Written on—within—my body.

The Scriptures, for me, are incorporated *bodily*. They are in my *corpus* like the blood in my veins. I do not always know what to make of or know how to understand this reality of scriptural incorporation or scriptural incarnation. But I have come to understand "the Word" that is hidden in my heart and that is incorporated into the fabric of who I am as a sign of, witness to, and manifestation of the presence of God through all the multiple and unfolding phases of my life.

Thus I return to the image of the road to Emmaus that hangs on my grandparents' dining room wall. In this story, Jesus appears to his friends as they travel along the road as a stranger who seems unaware or untroubled by the events of the preceding days. But then Jesus' friends invite the stranger to stay with them for the evening meal. And when he shares bread with them, they recognize Jesus in this stranger.

Jesus was the one with whom the disciples had shared so much time, and with whom they had invested so much energy. Yet, when he appears to them on the road to Emmaus, they do not initially recognize him and, like me, do not initially know what to do with him. But in their extension of hospitality toward this one that recent events had made strange to them, they are able to recognize their friend and teacher.

Friend and Teacher

Although Scripture is that friend with whom I have shared so much time and in whom I have invested so much energy, there was a time when, through *over*-use, *mis*-use, *ab*-use, and, probably, occasionally even untimely *non*-use, Scripture became the stranger to me. It was the unknown, unfamiliar, even hostile stranger on the road with whom I was *not* interested in conversing. But as I have matured out of my later adolescent post-Bible-memory period of a blatant rejection of, if not utter disdain for, Scripture, I have moved into the ability to think of Scripture as *informing* rather than *dictating* my life (and, hopefully, the life of the church). And now as I move into my professional life in the academy, where my pursuits lead me to reflect on how various strands of tradition—philosophical, ethical, ethnic, and religious, to name a few—inform all of our lives, I think of Scripture as one of these strands of "tradition" that informs my life. In this way, I am able to see Scripture not only as a childhood friend and teacher but also as a friend and teacher I continue to encounter as an adult.

Anthropologist Clifford Geertz has insisted that humans are meaning-making creatures whose creaturely task is to spin webs of signification. These webs of meaning serve as models of and models for how individuals understand reality.[2] Scripture is part of my web of signification and, more broadly speaking, Scripture is part of Mennonite webs of signification. It provides me—it gives the Mennonite church—a reference point *of* and a reference point *for* our postures in the world. Insofar, then, as Scripture has historically been part of this web of meaning that postures us, it deserves our attention.

We are well advised to be hospitable to the ways of making meaning that have served us throughout time—not because these things must continue to serve us in the same ways but because they have been our friends and teachers; because they are hidden in our hearts; and because, like it or not, they are part of how we construe, interpret and posture ourselves in the world. And perhaps in extending hospitality to these parts of who we have been, and of who we are, we can come to recognize and converse with our friend—not in the same form as before, but as friends transformed by the events in which we believe that the Spirit of God has been present.

Passages like "Vengeance is mine, I will repay, saith the Lord" (Rom. 12:19, KJV) and other stories of unspeakable atrocities committed by or in the name of God are still impossible for me to take at face value. They strike me as strange, awful, or even downright offensive. Some I am just uncomfortable with; still others are utterly beyond the scope of my imagination's ability to incorporate into the testimonies of God's peoples. Yet I am learning to read these stories. I am learning to read these things that are thoroughly offensive to my sensibilities about goodness and truth, and meanwhile, not to become bitter about the dissonance, even disgust, that I feel in their presence.

As I engage these passages, the encounter may be like that between utter strangers, not unlike the disciples' encounter with Jesus on the way to Emmaus. I am challenged to respond with hospitality to their strangeness—to walk with them, to listen to them, to sit with them, to break bread with them. I am challenged through this process to be drawn into the recognition of their beauty, their wildness, their terror, their power, or at very least, their historical significance for my faith tradition.

These words have been written on my forehead and hidden in my heart. Through this process of incorporation, I hear their call to faithfulness; toward the Word that is God.

Note

1. Unless otherwise noted, Scripture references in this chapter are from the *New International Version.*

2. Clifford Geertz, "Religion as a Cultural System," in *The Interpretation of Cultures* (New York: Basic Books, 1973): 87-125.

CHAPTER 2

Playing in the Mud

Chad Martin

When telling stories about my faith journey, I always have to start with my church experience growing up at Assembly Mennonite Church (AMC) in Goshen, Indiana. On the one hand, I sometimes feel as though I am living in the shadow of that congregational experience. On the other hand, I think the particularities of my childhood at AMC shape how I have responded to the world, the church, and God this far into my adulthood.

Grounded in Good Earth

I came of age in a congregation that encouraged me to create an open-minded framework for my experiences of church, Christian spirituality, and the Bible. This congregation recognized that each person is on a particular and special spiritual journey. AMC allowed room for people to ask questions and to walk their journeys at their own pace. As a youth, I saw the fact that congregational participants did not talk down to me, stifle me, or oversimplify difficult faith issues as having a great deal of integrity. And, crucial to the development of who I am today, Assembly showed me how to fully embrace women in every part of congregational life and leadership. Seemingly at every turn, AMC embodied the premise that there are many ways to be church.

Even the architectural context for the congregation's life embodied such a premise. When I was young, the group worshiped in a remodeled factory building (complete with an apartment rented to various members of the church). For Sunday school, my classes met in such places as "The Little House" (a three-room house totaling about 300 square feet that was actually rented to families before AMC owned it—complete with a scary basement); "The Brown House" (a nearly condemned house on the corner, whose second floor was completely off limits); and "Bertha's Basement" (obviously a basement, located a few blocks away and full of old furniture and graffiti created by members of our youth group in earlier days). These places had character, a character created over time by the collective experiences of those of us in the classes. I felt ownership in this church experience and in my faith and the Bible as well.

Of course my home church had its limitations, but I am grateful that it nurtured in me the ability to envision the possibility of many ways to be Christian and to experience the Bible. This nurturing established a realm of grace within which I have grown and changed without straying far from the fold of Christian community.

This is a tremendous gift. It means I have escaped some of the spiritual, emotional, and intellectual baggage that seems to weigh down so many folks on their journeys. The curse of this gift, though, is that I struggle not to take my faith for granted. I often feel like my journey is following a rather straight trajectory—relatively free of the mountains, ravines, and detours that make for a good traveling story. In telling my story, then, I must draw attention to the details. The compelling features of my voyage reveal themselves more in the subtleties along the way.

So here is my story. It is a kind of travelogue recording sights, sounds, and moments of grace with the Bible—my traveling companion I have enjoyed for some time.

The first moment comes from my baptism preparation classes. I had been asking many questions about homosexuality—about right and wrong, about ways to respond to gay and lesbian folks, about what God thinks of all this—and I turned to the Bible for answers. I recall this because I had rarely searched the Scriptures for answers to contemporary life issues before this time, and I have rarely done so with the same diligence since then.

While I did not realize it at the time, I see now that my pastor's responses to my questions were probably critical to broadening my view of Scripture. She responded with integrity: She shared her personal beliefs about human sexuality, she explained the congregation's understanding as an institution, she acknowledged a wide range of beliefs within the membership of AMC, and she was honest about difficult Scripture texts. Looking back on this encounter, I am not struck by any particular answer my pastor gave. Rather, I continue to be struck by her honesty and her openness to growth and new understanding.

Another encounter came each fall when the church embarked on a four-week study of a particular book of the Bible during a Sunday morning sermon series. I am sure this is not uncommon, but these studies sent me a signal about how to approach the Bible thoughtfully. The church often brought in guest preachers, including Bible professors from Goshen College and Associated Mennonite Biblical Seminary. I valued the seriousness with which the congregation was committed to reading the Bible beyond the face value of the text, looking for deeper, broader understanding. It showed me early in my spiritual development that one could read the Bible through the lens of a scholar, of a pastor, of a searching disciple. And this kind of intentional study showed me that each set of lenses could enlighten us and offer different insights to the whole community.

Grounded in the Written Word

One clear memory of my Goshen College years is of the time I attempted to read through the Bible during my Study Service Term in the Dominican Republic. This challenge was motivated primarily by the lack of other unread books in my suitcase. So, I thought, why not give the Bible a try. I tried reading page after page; I knew this might not be an effective approach, but again, why not? I think I got stuck somewhere in the middle of Deuteronomy. Perhaps all I learned through that experience is that there is much in the Bible that is unfamiliar to me, and I should not presume to know the book without a great deal more diligent study. Since then, I have talked with my grandmother and learned she has read the entire Bible about twenty times. I am inspired by her fortitude in this spiritual discipline. I respect the high premium she places on knowing the Scriptures, albeit in her own way. I hope to someday be able to say I too tried hard to know my Scripture.

I also participated in the Ministry Inquiry Program during college.[1] I was fortunate enough to preach three times. I discovered I love the preacher's task of digesting a particular text and struggling with it in preparation for trying to say something of value to a congregation. Of the three sermons I preached, the most meaningful one to me and many congregants was based on the text hardest for me to digest. I remember after two weeks of no insight walking into the pastor's office on Friday afternoon, fearing that the forty-eight hours left was hardly time enough for God to send a lightning bolt. The pastor assured me it would work out and that sermons often work on their own time. Of course it did work out. And I realized I get the most meaning from trying to draw ideas from what seem the most mysterious and challenging texts. I continue to love this kind of struggle.

The Elements of Scripture

More recently, I encountered the Bible in another meaningful form. In autumn 2002, I took a class on the historical books of the Old Testament at Pittsburgh Theological Seminary (PTS). As with my Bible classes at Goshen, this class kindled my enthusiasm for reading the Scripture through an academic lens. PTS has a well-funded archaeology program that organizes annual digs in Israel, and the archaeology professor taught my Old Testament class. His first three lectures were based on his many years of trips to Israel and consisted entirely of stories, slides, and pointing to places on maps. He established a geographic and physical context for our investigation of the text. This context connected with me immediately because I am a potter and I love geography. Many of his slides showed pots and sculptures created five thousand years ago.

My encountering these artifacts connected me to an historical stream of craftspeople and helped me recognize my place in the tradition of God's people. Encountering Scripture became much like making pots: When I fearlessly play in the mud and do not worry about the fire, beauty can come from material that others would consider too dirty to mess with.

All of this being said, what value do I now place on the Bible?

I think other believers who are part of my postmodern generation must make a choice if we are to make the Bible sacred. Our world is characterized by too much information. We are surrounded by television, the Internet, and even too many books. While I have several versions of the Bible on my bookshelf, these copies share space with literally hundreds of other books. I could just as easily view my copies of the Bible simply as ordinary texts, equal to all the books that surround it, or equal to all the information my head takes in every day. That means if the Bible is to be considered sacred, I must choose to make it sacred.

I suppose, though, that I am a bit of a traditionalist. I hold the Bible before me as the defining text for my spiritual journey. I think I am a better believer when I read it. I want my faith to be shaped by a biblical understanding of life and human existence. Despite many difficult passages, I still choose to believe that every part of the Bible reveals something about God and about humanity with potential to shape life for the better. I have read some feminist theology, some liberation theology, some sociology of religion, some right-wing fundamentalist thought, some arguments for a more pluralistic approach to spirituality and religion. All of these have shaped how I read the Bible. None of them has made me want to disown Scripture.

I hold the Bible up as a defining text because I believe it is a tool for meeting God. So here are ways I now try to use this tool to help me meet God.

I like to take my Bible with me every time I go to church. Hopefully this is not all self-righteousness. I try to actively read the texts used during the service. I think it helps me process what I experience there.

I like to juxtapose the Bible alongside ideas that seem to conflict with aspects of its teachings and authority. Some examples of the conflicts that I am referring to include evolution, gender equality, archaeological evidence that questions Old Testament history, dinosaurs, possible life on other planets, or sacred texts from other religions. Rather than trying to fit these extra-biblical ideas into the Bible or else throw them away, I think they need to be held together so they can inform each other. I think my faith is strongest when I try to employ as full an understanding of life, God, and the world as possible. This happens for me when I allow myself to question what I find in the Bible.

I like to contemplate the Bible in personal meditation. I find this extremely hard to do in my daily routine, so much so that I often question the value I think it holds for me. But I know that the few times in my life I have studied the Bible and prayed regularly, I have felt more grounded and closer to God.

I love to study the Bible academically. I enjoyed every class I took in the Bible, Religion, and Philosophy department at Goshen College.

And I look forward to similar study at the graduate level. I want to delve deeply into the biblical text. I want to know it as fully as I can. I do not want to take it for granted.

I like to read other spiritual texts that inform my faith as well as the Bible. Many contemporary authors, as well as historical ones, articulate truth. As a student of theology, I have of course been shaped significantly by contemporary Christian writers. John Howard Yoder's *The Politics of Jesus*, Donald Kraybill's *The Upside-Down Kingdom*, and Rudy Wiebe's *Blue Mountains of China* are works by Mennonites that have informed and added to my reading of the biblical text. Various theologies of liberation also have significantly informed my attitude toward the Bible, including works by Robert McAfee Brown, James Cone, Rosemary Radford Ruether, and Elisabeth Schüssler Fiorenza.

I like to balance the Bible against other places I meet God. Some of the other places where I encounter God are in human relationships, in the natural world, and the arts.

In many ways I feel like a novice approaching this complicated book. But I also like to think I have spent a great deal of time with it and that it has shaped me. I choose to keep the Bible with me as I continue my faith journey; this traveling companion makes my life richer.

Note

1. The Ministry Inquiry Program offers college students the opportunity to spend eleven weeks of their summer working in a congregation with the supervision of a pastor. Visitation, worship leading, preaching, participating in congregational board and committees, teaching classes, leading groups, outreach ministries, reading, and reflection are all part of the student's summer experience.

CHAPTER 3

Love, Peace, and Preconceptions

Jill Landis

Scripture for me has been something I have encountered, struggled with, and learned to embrace. As I consider the various life experiences I have had, I find several questions have persisted regarding the way I have approached the tasks of reading, understanding, and interpreting Scripture. What happens when we have in our minds a certain expectation or outcome about Scripture's meaning? Will we inevitably find basis and support for all of our theological assertions? Is it better to go to Scripture without our preconceived notions as to the meaning of its message? Is that even possible? I have not always been conscious of these questions while pondering and walking with Scripture, but they have shaped who and where I am today.

Encounters with Scripture

My journey with Scripture began on my grandmother's lap when I was two. "God is love," she would say, sing, and write. While I do not remember much more of the content of these initial theological lessons with my grandmother, I realize now that her actions said something about her journey with Scripture and set the stage for what was to become my own journey. Yet the belief that God is love has been a difficult one for me to grasp. I am not exactly sure when I began to doubt this basic notion that God is, in fact, love, but there came a point during my time at Eastern Mennonite University (EMU) in Harrisonburg, Virginia, when I knew I needed to be converted to the power of this conviction. What I did not know was that owning the belief in God's love would require an encounter with Scripture.

One summer during college I worked part-time as an intern for a Mennonite congregation in Sarasota, Florida. That experience was a watershed for me. Driving from my job at the dry cleaners to my internship one day, I took the matter into my own hands and issued God a challenge: "God, if you love me, prove it!" The time of questioning that followed became foundational for my basic understanding of Scripture's references to God's love for God's people. I began to seek out places in Scripture that spoke of God's love. The psalmists scream about God's faithful love that endures forever (Ps. 106, 118, 136). Both John's gospel and 1, 2, and 3 John are permeated with teachings about God's love and purpose for being. Romans 8:38-39 reveals God's vast love for us: "For I am convinced that neither death, nor life, nor angels, nor rulers, nor things present, nor things to come, nor powers, nor height, nor depth, nor anything else in all creation, will be able to separate us from the love of God in Christ Jesus our Lord." And then there is Jesus' question to Peter: "Simon, son of John, do you love me more than these?" With Peter's affirmative response, Jesus says to him, "Feed my lambs" (John 21:15).

That fall when I returned to EMU, all of my theological understandings seemed to crumble. The question of what it meant to say that I believe in the power of God's love still loomed large, but more nuanced questions about my faith also came into play. I began to ask about fundamental Christian teachings—such as, Is Jesus really the Son of God?

While I was not looking for answers, somehow I came across the story of Nehemiah. I was surprised to find that this story in Scripture connected with me, made a great deal of sense, and offered some sense of relief during a time of great confusion and loss. The temple had been destroyed and Nehemiah took it upon himself and the people of Israel to rebuild both the temple and the surrounding wall that were in ruins (Neh. 2:17–3:32). At the crux of a faith crisis, this is what I found myself doing. While my former faith and beliefs also lay in ruins, I was coming to the pile of rubble like Nehemiah, seeking to rebuild. I began to sort through the wreckage and separate out pieces I could use in my theological building project. Conclusions I had come to, such as "God does not love me," were tossed out and old foundational beliefs—the conviction that God is love—were re-set and became my new foundation.

In these two situations—demanding God's love reveal itself to me and finding my faith in ruins—I found myself going to Scripture because my life experiences were raising tough questions, and those questions needed thoughtful answers that could withstand the weight of heavy questions and doubts. Even though God had not spoken audibly to me about this deep, unending love for me, and since I was not being convinced by others, I specifically went to the Scriptures to find proof of God's love. And I found it. Amid a major faith crisis, I was simply looking for something I could believe, something that was true. That something was God's love for me, and it gave way to new clarity and personal growth.

Struggling with Scripture

I had begun to question Mennonite polity and practice in high school, and that process of questioning turned into a real wrestling and struggle with Scripture. I was in a baptism class when I first realized that Mennonite polity overruled childlike faith in God. I had expected that baptism would be a simple proclamation of my desire to follow God, profess my belief in Jesus, and commit myself to a faith journey. I soon discovered there was present what felt like a hidden agenda. Baptism was also about church membership—more specifically, becoming a member of my home congregation. This would not have been such a big deal, except that joining the membership of this particular congregation seemed to take on a focus all its own. "What if I don't want to be a member here?" I asked my pastor. This was unheard of; baptism and membership went together. I decided at that point to forgo baptism. I was not ready to adhere to the rule of church membership.

Unfortunately, this experience soured my understanding of theological discourse. The people I turned to with my questions seemed to resist them and to give me trite and closed answers. There did not seem to be a willingness to engage a young theologian in these questions of Mennonite polity. I wanted to know how Scripture played into this basic but seemingly crucial theological belief about church membership. I went to the church looking for answers but was given a copy of *Confes-*

sion of Faith in a Mennonite Perspective (Scottdale, Pa.: Herald Press, 1995).

In contrast to that experience, at EMU there was an environment in which questions could be asked and explored without running the risk of being told one was wrong for suggesting a certain idea or coming to a conclusion different from the status quo. While I was already asking questions of myself and my church in private, my professors provided a space where I finally felt the freedom and permission to ask those questions publicly. I also felt a genuine invitation to dialogue with others about their questions and faith journeys.

Comparing my home congregation to my college classes, I found myself making an observation that troubled me: Mennonite theology, while rooted in Scripture, looks to Scripture with a specific outcome in mind. I was not looking for a specific answer in regard to church membership but was asking a specific question. Instead of being encouraged to explore what Scripture might say about my question, I was asked to adhere to the conclusions others had already reached.

My struggle to reconcile my questions with Scripture and Mennonite theology continued. This struggle became quite intense while I was completing a take-home test for a theology class during my second year of college. One question asked us to give our theological perspective on women in ministry. I remember agonizing over this in my room for hours. I had grown up with women in the pulpit and who were pastors, but now, for the first time, I was confronted with classmates who thought the point of view that women should fulfill such roles was wrong. My peers simply offered another perspective, but it was different enough from what I was used to that it caused me to search out what Scripture had to say with a keener eye.

I began to find Scriptures that deterred women from being involved in ministry and held them down as men's inferiors in carrying out the responsibilities of the church. What happened in the course of my working out an answer to this question was pure emotional struggle. Scripturally, if women were not allowed to be in ministry, where did that leave me? Where did that leave the female pastors and mentors who surrounded me as I had grown up, many of whom had ministered to me, encouraging me to become a minister in my own right?

Unfortunately, I no longer have that paper to look back over and see what I wrote then. But I remember agonizing over the question and my struggle to find a biblical basis for my belief that women were indeed called and encouraged to be in ministry in the church. I went to my professor later and informed him about my struggle, asked him questions, and eventually came to a point of scriptural understanding that supported my belief that women could and should be in ministry. This experience brings me back to the question I raised at the outset: What happens when we have in our minds a certain expectation or outcome about Scripture's meaning?

I also found that this question is especially pertinent in dealing with topics like peace. I had already been "properly" taught about Mennonite views on war and peace, but I had determined that I needed to figure out for myself the truth about peace in the Bible. This desire coincided with an opportunity to create a curriculum to teach peacemaking to high school youth. I looked up passages of Scripture, sorted through resources, and read all kinds of books. I talked with some of my professors and inevitably came back to the traditional Mennonite peace stance. But, because I was exploring the question of peace with the intention of teaching high school youth and I also had to teach them the Mennonite perspective on peace, I felt my vision was slightly skewed.

How do we reconcile war and violence in the Old Testament with the New Testament understanding of peace? What about Christian denominations that do not adhere to the kinds of peace teachings Mennonites profess to believe? These were natural and obvious questions that surfaced during my research and study. Yet I knew I eventually had to make sure these questions were met with "Mennonite" answers, even though my intentions had been to explore all the topics at hand without falling back on predictable outcomes. Again, will we inevitably find basis and support for our theological assertions?

Embracing the Spirit Through Scripture

There is one thing in Scripture that I have been able to explore without the "interference" of Mennonite theology: the Holy Spirit. In all of my years in the church, I had not remembered much reference to the Holy Spirit at all. But a woman who was informally mentoring me at the end of high school became the first person to introduce me to the Holy Spirit. Her references to the Holy Spirit were rooted more in the charismatic tradition, but I was fascinated. Everything was so new!

It was through this woman's tutelage that I began to learn about various spiritual disciplines like fasting and more about the gifts of the Holy Spirit. This awakening was instrumental in my own discovery and search for answers regarding the work and role of the Holy Spirit in the Christian life. Since a Mennonite perspective on the Holy Spirit was not ingrained in me like the peace position was, I was free to ask questions and seek out answers without the hindrance of a "traditional Mennonite stance" or preconceived interpretation of Scripture. I was fascinated to learn about movements attributed to the Holy Spirit throughout church history, specifically in early twentieth-century America. I even found some cases in Mennonite history where there was a more active connection between the church and the life of the Holy Spirit. For this reason, I was also disappointed to see that the unpredictable and charismatic influence of the Holy Spirit seemed to be resisted or simply not mentioned in many of my present-day Mennonite circles.

While it felt exciting to be doing something that seemed radical—looking at the Scriptures in light of my questions about the Holy Spirit—I also felt very alone. I knew some in the church would meet my questions and new presuppositions with ridicule, so I was left to explore my questions within a small segment of the Mennonite population. Today, I continue to figure out ways to reconcile my understandings about the Holy Spirit with mainstream Mennonite understandings. But two questions linger: Is it better to go into Scripture with no assumptions about what we will find? Is that even possible?

Integrating Experiences with Scripture

In recent years a number of events have caused my personal life to intersect with my interaction with Scripture. One has been the challenge of writing devotional material for a Mennonite audience. Writers are asked to take specific Scripture passages and make them not only inspirational but applicable and relevant to readers' daily lives. Once again, I have had to go to Scripture with a specific purpose, audience, and task in mind. This has been much different from other types of theological discourse I have been engaged in, but even devotional writing must be scrutinized by my questions about how we approach Scripture.

Second is the experience I have had in "fasting" from Scripture for a year. My inadvertent and later conscious decision to fast from reading

Scripture was necessitated by a difficult experience. I had sensed God's call to ministry in the church, but after pouring my heart and soul into my work, I became burnt out. I had been looking for God and even expecting God to be obviously present as I responded to my call. Instead, I felt somewhat abandoned and extremely exhausted. Where had God been amid it all? I had no desire to go looking for God in Scripture, and I abandoned my usual practice of journal writing. I had spent fifteen years finding new and amazing things in Scripture; now the text suddenly became dry and useless. The best remedy seemed to be continuing my fast from Scripture.

Two things resulted from this year-long fast. First, I found new ways to journal and communicate some of these thoughts and struggles. Second, I came back to Scripture with a fresh and renewed desire to soak it up. Perhaps this was because I returned to Scripture without any agenda, without any intentions other than to hear and listen to what God might be saying to me.

Renewed Encounter, Struggle, and Embrace

More recently I have had the privilege of teaching Sunday school to bright and energetic grade school students. The experience presented an unexpected set of challenges. How do you teach basic (yet abstract) Christian beliefs such as trusting in God, resurrection, and "God is love" when the curriculum focuses on the more concrete by telling stories? How do you present a theology of prayer when all you really want to communicate is that God is not a "prayer genie" who grants our every wish—like getting that new set of Legos for Christmas? What do you do with the children's hard questions?

Teaching Sunday school has forced me to learn how to explain the concepts of Scripture and Mennonite faith in very basic and simple ways. The children in my class are malleable. Because they are not as invested in Mennonite theology as I was, everything they encounter in our lessons is fresh, new, and exciting. Through my time with the children, I am realizing a very basic thing: Our journey with Scripture is about learning the basic concepts of faith without pretense or predetermined theological outcomes.

So, what happens when we have in our minds a certain expectation or outcome about Scripture's meaning? Will we inevitably find basis and support for all of our theological assertions? Is it better to go to Scripture without preconceived notions as to the meaning of its message? Is that even possible? These questions persist. So it seems to me to be in our best interest to model ourselves after my young Sunday school students who approach Scripture not with specific answers in mind but with honest questions. Doing so will allow us all to experience the freedom of striving to understand what is at the heart of God's work and movement both throughout Scripture and in our world.

CHAPTER 4

Traveling over Land, Through Water, in the Spirit

Bethany Spicher Schonberg

As the rain and the snow
come down from heaven,
and do not return to it
without watering the earth
and making it bud and flourish,
so that it yields seed for the sower and bread for the eater,
so is my word that goes out from my mouth:
It will not return to me empty,
but will accomplish what I desire
and achieve the purpose for which I sent it.
—Isaiah 55:10-11

Every day at rush hour I ride my bike from the Mennonite Central Committee (MCC) Washington Office on Capitol Hill to the MCC Voluntary Service Unit in Mount Pleasant. I cut across New Jersey Avenue, left on S Street to Ninth Street, up Florida Avenue to Eleventh Street, catch Columbia to Sixteenth. Every day it's a miracle I get home alive.

Pigeons bank and dive above the intersections. One lands on a roof, blinks its bright eye, walks right off the edge of the building, and plummets two stories before it spreads its wings. A high school marching band stands on a corner blasting "We will, we will rock you." A dead rat curls on the sidewalk like it's sleeping. A grandmother with a broom sweeps the grass in front of her house. I catch a whiff of honeysuckle. A sign outside a church reads, "Love or perish." A siren blares. A firecracker sparks, small boys scream and scatter. A woman cries, "Roses, roses," at the passing cars. I cross against a red light, too late, my mind whirrs, I turn suddenly. Much squealing and honking, a head out the window: "Girl, you keep that up, you gonna . . . ," but I don't hear the rest. A sparrow darts up out of nowhere trailing a long ribbon of toilet paper in its beak. A man comes toward me on a bike, standing on the pedals, sweating, pumping hard, and wailing, "I got a pocket full of stones." Over and over again. "A pocket full of stones."

I watch my legs clench up the hill on Eleventh Street. I write haikus in my head. I practice Morse code on the handlebars. I try to sing all five verses of "Be Thou My Vision." I think of the e-mails I got today. Congress is debating the Child Tax Credit. My friend is throwing a birthday party. I think of an article I read. There's a whole community of farmers in Cambodia with their limbs blown off by landmines: the ones with legs help the ones with arms and vice-versa. I think of the lectionary passage ft one of them will fall to the ground apart from the will of your Father" (Matt. 10:29).

It all swirls together, and I'm almost home. Tghe wind's in my face, and all down the block maple keys are falling, spinning in the summer light. I close my eyes, let the wind carry me. And I pray Isaiah's desperate prayer, "Oh, that you would rend the heavens and come down, that the mountains would tremble before you" (Isa. 64:1, NIV). I lift my bike up the front steps and calculate the hours I'll spend riding before the end of the year: 245.

Inside, I drop my bike, grab my journal, write it all down. For years now I've thought, "If I can just get it on paper, the pieces of my life between the covers of a book, then . . . well, then something will happen."

Assignment to self:

> Write it all down in a roar of waters, scream my head off, yell that I'm drowning, then emerge in the end, dripping but poised, perfect, without a ripple.
>
> Wonder about others who've had similar aspirations, namely the writers of the Word of God.
>
> Watch the lights. Keep an eye on the traffic. Don't get hit by a bus.

I

My family and I read straight through the Bible, a chapter a night for ten years. We took turns reading the verses out loud, stumbling over the Old Testament names, blushing through the stories. The fat king Eglon killed by a left-handed man (Judg. 3:15-23); Lot's daughters offered to the men of Sodom (Gen. 19:6-8). As I recall we weren't allowed to watch the Smurfs on television. "Too violent," my parents said. Summers after breakfast, Dad would read the day's Proverb and hand out the chore lists. To this day I can't sleep in without thinking that poverty will likely overtake me like a bandit.

All the while, I was memorizing for stickers in Sunday school—whole Psalms, chapters from John and Romans, most times from a little red King James Version: "He restoreth my soul" (Ps. 23:3). "His only begotten son" (John 3:16). I'll be saying "Our Father [who] art in heaven" (Matt. 6:9a, KJV) until the kingdom comes; I can't help it. But deeper in my psyche than the words in that Bible are the colored pictures I inspected over Cheerios in church: the head of Goliath spurting blood, the woman at the well with a jar on her hip, the empty tomb overgrown with lilies.

II

Say you're a member of one of the Twelve Tribes any time after the Promised Land but before the Messiah. Your people will stand outside for days to hear the Word read aloud. You have verses on your doorpost, maybe even on your forehead. You have priests who kiss the Scriptures if they're dropped, who won't step on a scrap of paper for fear it contains a word from the Lord. You have prophets running around who smash clay jars in the street, who bury their underwear, who tell you the Babylonians are coming to rip you to shreds. You learn to cope. You eat unleavened bread, mourn in sackcloth, and take your pets to the temple altar.

Your word for "word" is *dabar*, which also means "thing," "event," "deed," or "act." And you have seen words happen: you have seen blessings and curses work. In the recent memory of your people, God did crazy things with water, fire, and locusts. Everyone's afraid. The name of your God is unpronounceable. Your best friend is ceremonially unclean. You worry that there's mildew on your wall. There are so many rules to remember. You decide you had better make a list, write them down.

III

In junior high, I started reading the Bible on my own, against all odds. I had a purple Bible designed and published just for teenagers with special fold-out sections like "Hot Topic #7: Abstinence!" I had a series of awkward Sunday school teachers who would ask things like "How do you think the leper felt after Jesus healed him?" then look desperately to me and my sister. Of course, we would answer after the awful silence, and so the charade continued week after week. Incredibly, through it all, I clung to my Bible, finding in it protection and proof that my public high school in central Pennsylvania, Huntingdon Area, was the kingdom of darkness. And that parties were so bad that even if I ever were actually invited, I could not go.

At Laurelville Mennonite Church Center, where I went to summer camp, the Bible was cool. My friends and I mailed letters to each other all year long and looked through the concordance for verses like "I can do all things through Christ who strengthens me" (Phil. 4:13, NKJV) to write on the envelopes with markers. We started Bible study groups at our "pagan" high schools and sent reports of our efforts to each other like young apostles.

I did what I called "devotions" most mornings: I had this idea that you could open the Bible to any page, read it for five minutes before you caught the bus, and all that day, boys would like you and you would get A's. When I was a senior, I picked Jeremiah 29:11 NIV for my yearbook quote: "'For I know the plans I have for you,' declares the LORD, 'plans to prosper you and not to harm you, plans to give you hope and a future.'" Everyone else had lines from Bon Jovi songs, and I felt that I had entered the fire.

IV

Say you're God. You don't say so many words, but when you do, suns explode and continents heave—then there was that time it started raining. "Something's got to change," you think to yourself. You have a group of stiff-necked people on your hands. You thought you'd keep it simple, but the Ten Commandments did not come off so well. So now you put everything on paper for them *twice*, but they still could not make it all the way through to one Jubilee. They got themselves hauled off by the Babylonians, now they're writing about these wars like they were your idea. The prophets are not working; there is Ezekiel right now, lying on his side, cooking with cow manure. You wonder how they strayed so far from the garden. You wonder how to so love the world. You wonder what it's like to be made for eternity and caught in time and space. You think you'd better try another kind of word.

V

Eastern Mennonite University (EMU, Harrisonburg, Va.)would, I knew, be like four years of summer camp with tests. I was wrong; it was better. My first year, I thought I'd landed in the kingdom of light. I joined all the clubs, I never missed a chapel, I adored my classes, and the Bible positively exploded. I thrilled at Walter Wink's new interpretation of turning cheeks and claimed creative pacifism for myself once and for all. I raged against abstract concepts like globalization and substituted "corporations" for "enemies" all through the prophets. I read the psalms the way I read poetry: "deep calls to deep" (Ps. 42:7), "righteousness and peace kiss each other" (Ps. 85:10).

In chemistry class, atomic attraction blew me away: What holds the electron to the nucleus? What keeps it from careening into space? Colossians 1:17 NIV became my mantra: "[Christ] is before all things, and in him all things hold together." Every morning I woke up sure that I was zeroing in on the secret of life, certain that today was the day that I would arrive.

VI

Say you're Jesus. You're the Word God spoke, with a capital W—the thing, the event, the deed, the act. But your mom was pregnant out of wedlock, your dad's a construction worker, and you grow up in Galilee like a regular kid. You learn the old words by heart, but even at twelve you shock your teachers with new interpretations. When you're thirty, you start talking to people. You talk to men who fish for a living, tax collectors, lepers, children, and women at wells. Mostly you tell stories about seeds and sheep. You also say things like, "Get up, take your mat, and go home!" (Mark 2:11) and "Lazarus, come out!" (John 11:43). And you talk about yourself a lot saying, "I am the bread of life" (John 6:35), and "I am the light of the world" (John 8:12). It only takes three years of talking to get yourself crucified, and in your death you speak the words you came to say: "Forgive them" (Luke 23:34).

It's enough to hide the sun, shake the earth, and knock the socks off the Israelites one last time. And through it all, the earnest disciples snooze through the sermons, miss the miracles, wake when it's all over to hit each other and holler, "Someone better have taken notes on what he just said!"

VII

My friends returned from their cross-cultural experiences in Latin America or the Middle East hairy and tanned, suitcases full of ethnic souvenirs in hand, and all kinds of angst about organized religion, which, as far as I could tell, was remedied by skipping chapel, adding a philosophy minor, and smoking pot. I'd gone to Kansas for a year, instead. I met some farmers, planted some seeds, drove my car into the sunset on those long straight prairie roads, and praised the Lord.

Coming back to the mountains of Virginia and finding my friends had turned to alcohol and agnosticism broke my heart. So I wrote manifestos for chapel and the *Weather Vane,* our campus newspaper, pleading with my peers to see that Jesus was a revolutionary and redeemer; maybe I was trying to convince myself as much as anyone. I hit my friends with all the verses about atoms and flowers and justice, even quoted some cosmic Colossians.

Looking back, I'm not sure what I was after exactly. Maybe a campus-wide group hug. Maybe the big sister in me wanted to bring everyone along, keep us all talking and happy. Now my friends are all over the world busy with kingdom work, full of faith, some more orthodox than others, granted, but they are happy. And to think I'd have moved us to a little commune after college if I could have—somewhere in the Shenandoah Valley to can quarts of homemade applesauce and sing hymns for the rest of our lives. It would have been awful.

VIII

Say you're the early church any time after the Ascension and before the pope. You're not certain that Jesus is gone for good; there for awhile he kept showing up around suppertime. You hope to God he meant what he said about coming back soon because it's been hard without him. Washing feet and sharing money with all these people you don't like. Caring for the orphans and widows, healing the sick, casting out demons—all the while never knowing when God's going to sic the Holy Spirit on you and your friends.

Meanwhile, you know you're supposed to be going therefore into all the world, but your friends who try it get shipwrecked, beaten, and thrown to the lions. Even when they make it home alive, the converts backslide like you would not believe. Heretics are coming out of the woodwork all up and down the empire. Controversial manuscripts are being canonized right and left. What's more, the whole business is an administrative nightmare. All your friends want to get books named after them, so they're all writing letters, calling meetings, and nobody is left to make copies or take minutes. Somebody's got to organize this thing.

IX

So here I am alive, a quarter-century now, making my home in a city where pigeons wheel in intersections, where power and poverty exist side by side, where the language I have learned is inadequate. I could live for life in this neighborhood and never get it right. Remember the man with the pocket full of stones? Turns out he's singing about cocaine. Any child on the street could tell me that, of course; they could probably also sing anything by the Underground Kings (Pimp C and Bun B), even without the parental guidance advised.

Most days, all I can do is ask questions: What the heck does it mean that the Word dwells in me richly? Why do Mennonites not advocate for immigrants and against tax cuts unless I back it with the Bible? What do our Mount Pleasant neighbors think of us MCCers with our hymn sings and picnics on the porch? How does my reading the lectionary at night when I'm weary change my wild bike rides home? Why did I cry when I read last week "All things are yours . . . all are yours, and you are of Christ, and Christ is of God" (1 Cor. 3:21-23 NIV)? Why did I squelch the joyful urge to open my window and shout it down the block?

X

Say you're Planet Earth. Tides swell and clouds swirl. Zoom out, and there are the stars. Zoom in, and there is dewy grass, spider webs and grains of sand. Zoom in some more, and there are the atoms. The Word is all around you. You have confidence that it will go forth, as promised, like the rain and the snow, but you have some questions about the metaphor. The water system, see, is not tidy. It is not efficient. The seas rise and mountains crash, rivers change course and wipe out entire villages, it rains for months on end in Washington, D.C. and everyone gets grumpy. "Lord, have mercy." There is no consideration here for the small or the fragile. There is no guarantee where all that water will end up, what will flourish and what will parch, only that everything will die and rot, recombine, wash out to sea, and rise to rain again.

But for all your complaining, despite the wildness and wetness and seemingly endless circularity, on some days, when the wind is just right, you get the sense that something very large and very present is taking down the particulars: fallen sparrows, faded flowers, the hairs on the heads of women and men. There is a story here with a plot that's spinning itself out in every atom, repeating itself in grasses and stones, wanting to be told again and again, each time a little more. People in every century, on every continent, are listening for it, getting it wrong, crumpling the paper, trying again. Across the globe, forests are falling for all those rough drafts.

XI

I think that's enough splashing about for today, enough treading water. All things are mine, yes, but here's my confession: I can't name all the animals, pluck up every weed, and it looks like I can't even tell the kids on my block what these stones mean. Might as well forget the perfect surfacing, no ripples. I can barely keep my head above water. I try to read the Word, try to step out on the street, and it's a headlong plunge—birds dart up out of nowhere, stars fall, sirens wail, mud flies everywhere.

I guess the closest I've come is that day my family biked home in the loudest, drowning-est thunderstorm ever to hit Phoenix, Arizona. The streets were flooded up to our pedals, the rain was stinging our eyes, we were gasping for breath, but we were grinning like fools—because Mom and Dad and God were right there with us, because the whole crazy enterprise had been their idea from the start.

I guess that's how it's been, at least for me. I guess all I can say is, "Come on out. The water's fine."

CHAPTER 5

Claiming God's Story as My Own

Jeremy Garber

Three is a magic number. Scholars and priests have claimed trinitarian faith for Christianity for nearly seventeen centuries. The ancient Greeks saw human beings divided into body, mind, and spirit, with each separate part conjoined to create the miracle of human consciousness. Recent inspired studies in psychology, biology, and sociology reveal that our selves are complicated threads of flesh, mind, and will, weaving inextricably throughout our interactions with other complicated beings.

So too, our journeys with Scripture take at least three parts. We find the Bible enfleshed in story, the nuts and bolts of Hebrew and Greek, David and Jesus, falling away and returning to God. We use our minds—our powers of discernment and creation a little less than God's—to peer into God's stories and apply them to our own everyday situations. And we rely on the continuing power of the Spirit to move us to further storytelling and reflection that write new pages of Scripture every day.

The Picture Bible and the Story

My most vivid personal evidence for the multi-sensory storytelling extravaganza that is Scripture came in the form of an Easter present— *The Picture Bible,* written by Iva Hoth and illustrated by Andre le Blanc.

Still in print (Elgin, Ill.: Chariot Books, 1978), the cover reads, "The Timeless Stories of the Bible in Full Color!" complete with a grimly Charlton Hestonesque Moses and a long-haired caucasian Jesus straight from Warner Sallman's traditional portrait. *The Picture Bible* attempted to transfer the bold lines and vivid colors of comic book illustration to the biblical message at the expense of some notable amount of detail. It worked for me; *The Picture Bible* was my canonical evidence that Peter wore a purple-and-black-striped tunic. I devoured it greedily until the binding wore out.

The Picture Bible did not provide a new translation, or even a paraphrase. It lacked significant portions of text and therefore the complex poetry of the original languages. However, the vivid illustrations and exclamation-point-studded text drove the stories of the Bible inside the fledgling reader's mind. Rather than speak a language 4,000 or 400 years dead, *The Picture Bible* distilled biblical narrative into its action-packed essence. This narrative distillation provided the physical essence of ingesting the biblical story, the meat of the three-course dinner of integrating sacred text.

But a story without a reader lies on the page like lifeless mud in the Garden of Eden. Theology is the story, the framework that allows us to understand and interpret the stories of the Bible in a way relevant to our historical time and place. My childhood church's philosophy of Christian education subconsciously shaped my picture of the Bible. In fact, my introduction to theology began with an olive-green felt puppet who introduced the Bible story to us every Sunday. The puppet told us that Jesus teaches us that God loves us and expects us to love others as we are loved. These broad themes were wrapped around stories about Jesus gathering the children to him, Noah's ark, and Daniel in the lions' den. The God I learned about through these stories was a God of love, forgiveness, and protection; that God was incarnated for us through the narratives of the Bible. Just as Jesus taught clothed in human flesh, theology for us was enfleshed through childhood storytelling.

This elementary theology did not ignore the biblical text. We learned the order of the books and how to find a book when someone called out a reference. I remember visiting my grandmother's evangelical church in Michigan and winning the Bible memory drill, proudly bringing home a plaster statue as a trophy. But in addition to patchwork verses lifted out of context, my own congregation—College Mennonite

Church in Goshen, Indiana—taught me the grand story of God's liberation and salvation. The teachings of my church were centered on God expressed in Jesus through the Gospels, especially Jesus' teachings in the Sermon on the Mount.

As the first Gulf War mounted in the early 1990s, the elders of my home congregation helped us adolescents express our convictions about the Prince of Peace based on biblical themes and passages. I once volunteered to be interviewed for a "trial draft board" meeting at the church. Afterward, the church member who had played the role of draft board overseer said to me, "You did an excellent job. You really know your Bible." That affirmation was a source of pride in my knowledge of God's way—humble Mennonite pride, of course.

Using our Minds, Drawing on God's Spirit

Body and mind do not accomplish anything without willpower to apply them. Teachers and pastors had encouraged me about my knowledge—but had never encouraged me to consider using my biblical knowledge in my vocation. In college I started off as an English major and switched to theater; it soon became clear that my childhood years at church taught me far more about the Bible than did my college education. All the while, during those late adolescent years, I kept feeling that maybe this religion stuff really did not apply anymore. I stopped going to church and fell in with the rebellious theater party crowd. Yet all the time, the Bible was present in my memory. It was not the only book involved in my search for truth—I also searched through Buddhist texts, Sufism, and even pagan and occult books. Yet somehow I always came back to the stories of Jesus Christ ingrained into me during my youth. The God whom Jesus knew intimately simply made the most sense to me.

A particular church and particular pastors awakened the third corner of the biblical triangle—my willpower, my desire, my joy, God's Spirit. It takes love and community to be able to apply the body of the story and the theology of the mind. As I (unsuccessfully) tried to establish an acting career in Minneapolis, Minnesota, I began to attend a progressive urban church not out of religious conviction but out of loneliness. The young adult group at Faith Mennonite Church fed me socially and spiritually. Most important, pastors Patrick Preheim and Patty Friesen invited me to their house for board games and long talks. As we took the bus to rock concerts, the pastors listened to my struggles and offered me counsel and reflection. I credit these church leaders and a truly nurturing community for reawakening my love for the church and for the Bible. I could find fun and intelligent people who understood me and my search for God, and help me find it in the Bible of my childhood.

Evangelical Christians often critique progressive Christians for promoting the social gospel while ignoring the personal. The pastors at my urban, progressive congregation challenged me to develop an authentic personal spirituality as well as social commitment. I started a daily Bible journal during my time in the city. Each day I picked a chapter from the Old Testament and one from the New, wrote down my favorite verse from each chapter, and tried to explore why those verses or stories spoke to me. This meditation continues today. These fresh encounters with the biblical text help me develop my theology more explicitly as well as reacquaint me with specific biblical passages.

During my last month in Minneapolis, as I wrestled with what God was calling me to do with my life, my chapter for the day was Jeremiah 29. Verse 11 reads, "'For surely I know the plans I have for you,' says the Lord, 'plans for your welfare and not for harm, to give you a future with hope.'" That verse reassured and comforted me that God did indeed have a plan for me and that it was a good one. This particular chapter and verse, certainly out of context in its application to me, was a needed drop of refreshment during a difficult time.

I returned to my hometown of Goshen, Indiana and another progressive church community—Assembly Mennonite Church—which used its gifts of discernment to name my gifts and call me to use them in the church. I began attending Associated Mennonite Biblical Seminary (AMBS), and it was without a question the place I am meant to be. I love being with other scholars and future church leaders who have a fierce love for the story of Scripture. I love sweating over an earnest translation of ancient Hebrew. I love using my acting gifts to proclaim God's story, and my directing gifts to lead people to God in fresh and vibrant ways. Most of all, I love being a scholar of the most important texts in human history.

Combining the Universal and the Particular

My time at AMBS also led me to an understanding of the value of the universal story of God's salvation and our very personal encounters with God's text in our lives and in the world. I studied liberation theology in Guatemala in January 2003, awed by the sincere faith of its founders, enraged at the poverty I saw at the hands of American economic and military policies, overjoyed by the people I saw. One weekend we stayed with Guatemalan families in the village of Carranza comprised of dirt roads and tin roofs. I spoke no Spanish and tried to convey meaning through French cognates and wild hand gestures. How could I communicate? One sixteen-year-old managed to figure out I was studying the Bible. He recited a memorized verse in Spanish aloud, reference and all. I flipped to the passage in my English Bible and read it aloud. The ancient words of Scripture passing back and forth between us in our fragmented tongues. It was a magical moment.

So how do all of my human stories—body, mind, and spirit—shape my encounter with the overarching God story found in Scripture? I encounter Scripture as narrative—a gripping plot with fascinating characters wrestling with the most important issues of humanity. In Scripture, God writes the story of humanity through all-too-human flesh. The people who wrote God's story, though, were not some kind of divine typewriters blindly spewing forth what was channeled through them. They were particular people in particular places during particular times; each of their situations colored how they encountered what God was bringing to them.

Some readers find the use of historical-critical method scary or offensive; instead, it can prompt us to name God in our own lives. In the same way that God chose to dwell in a particular first-century Jewish prophet, God moves through our small individual lives, creating particular stories that weave together in the story of God's love and salvation through history.

Christian faith, then, affirms that the God story is real. Our discipleship means injecting our story into the God story, revealed to us through Scripture and particularly in Jesus' life as recorded in the Gospels. The stories of the Bible—the flesh of the God story—reveal the good and bad of human existence, as all good literature ought; we learn by both positive and negative example. But since particular, fallible people wrote the stories of the Bible in historical time, we need to use our minds to discern which examples are positive and universal and which are negative and time-specific.

Historical and literary studies help us do this; my minor in English literature has contributed immensely to my study of the Bible. And the community of discernment provides the key of the Holy Spirit that moves us to interpret the God story authentically here and now. We bring our particular gifts and experiences together, tell our small stories of God working in our lives, and together allow God's Spirit to lead us in interpreting the Bible in a way that is relevant to our time, place, and situation.

The Bible is God's story, but the story does not stop with the Bible. God's story continues in the church today, around the world and in our communities. And the Scriptures are not the only story through which God speaks. God speaks in literature and movies, in Flannery O'Connor and Andrew Lloyd Webber. God speaks in hand puppets and cartoon depictions of Peter. The Bible is not a science text, and it is not a legal document. It is a story made up of stories, the story of God trying to help us be the people God wants us to be in our little corner of creation. I am proud to claim that story as my own.

CHAPTER 6

Seeking Faith and Yearning for Love Beyond the Boundaries

Alicia Miller

My journey with Scripture is best told as my journey toward religious identity. My youth was spent in a traditional Mennonite church, one with liberal leanings given its urban context. In my midteens, as my family underwent major changes and growing experiences, my faith did as well. I ended up at the edge of the church, if not outside it. Since then, I have begun a quest to reconcile my life experiences with my faith, and this includes my relationship with Scripture.

As my family and faith both fell apart and then fell together again, Gandhi, Rumi, Simone Weil, Thich Nhat Hanh, and Rainer Maria Rilke were some of the many thinkers I turned to when I felt an estrangement from my own tradition's text. I lament my lost relationship with the Bible and Jesus as simple "keys to the kingdom." Today, though, I find myself embracing the same Christian ideals I was raised with. I find them in many sources, many Scriptures, and therefore desire a more universal name for my faith.

In the Beginning

Among my earliest Scripture memories is a little Alicia diligently memorizing Bible verses at church, moments before reciting them in

Sunday school, then placing a star on the sticker chart. By third grade, I had begun earnestly learning the basic tenets of Mennonite belief so that I could explain to people who I was. I learned that I was different when I had to stand up in class and explain why I would not say the Pledge of Allegiance. That same year, I began a series of theological discussions on the bus with a science-loving nerd named Alex. One day he asked, "If God created everything, then why is there bad in the world?" I took the question to heart and felt responsible to answer his challenge. We had a heated discussion without resolution. Only after I got off the bus did I triumphantly come up with the answer that God did not create the bad in the world but people chose to do bad, and that was sin; bad things are people's fault, not God's.

Over time I felt increasingly caught up in my faith. During a sixth-grade sleepover with my best friend, curled up in sleeping bags on couches in my game room, I casually told her what I had learned from church: as a Jew, she was going to hell if she did not accept Jesus. It was not the last time I would counsel her in error: I also tried to teach her how to flirt with boys, and most recently I have tried to impress upon her my views of the Israeli-Palestinian conflict. However, the tragedy of that first declaration has never left my mind. Fortunately for me, she laughed and said she did not believe in hell. That saved our relationship and also opened up for me the possibility that hell's existence could be debated.

Shortly thereafter, when I heard that our Catholic friend believed in something called purgatory, I knew that someone, somewhere, had to be making things up. Though without language to describe it at the time, it was becoming clear to me that at least part of my faith was socially constructed.

Nonetheless, I still had strong beliefs in right and wrong and deep convictions about Jesus and God's goodness. Once, in the middle of middle school, I remember that I stopped and thanked God for my blessed life.

Then "real life" started. At the end of eighth grade, a church member picked me up from my basketball game to tell me that a loved one had tried to commit suicide. I remember staring out the front window of his pickup truck in silence. I knew my view of the world would never be the same again. Yet nothing ever moved me more than listening to that family member play "Amazing Grace" in my living room during our next encounter weeks later. That combination of person and song was a religious text impressed forever on my heart.

But even that passionate hymn was not enough to carry the tune of the church in my life. The following years unveiled more family dysfunctions, including my parents' looming divorce and the reality of depression among us. Amid this thundering, trapped in the car with my brothers on a road trip to Goshen, two of my older brothers asked, "Why would you even think there was a God?" I did not have an answer. And with that, my childlike faith flew right out the window, discarded on Highway 31 somewhere between Kokomo and Nappanee.

I began to look at my brothers' question more deeply as my family fell apart, individually and corporately. It seemed as if we were competing to check off the list of things that could go wrong in Midwestern families. I no longer thanked God for my "perfect life."

My next encounter with religious texts would come from school instead of the church that I attended less and less. In my senior English literature class, my teacher posed the question, "What is Good and what is Evil?" I loved it. I argued one way and another until I said that Good is everything creative and Evil is everything else. I was thrilled; it drew me back to the exhilaration of my fourth-grade discussions with Alex. The texts we examined were two versions of the creation story (two texts of one story being another eye-opener to me). In one version, God gave the idea of free will. This, combined with my brothers' question, drew God down to a personal level—tying God's existence to free will.

A second and more pivotal theological struggle in high school came in a weekly Bible study with some of my senior girlfriends. There I wrestled with Jesus' words recorded in John 14:6: "No one comes to the Father except through me." Still haunted by my sixth-grade words to my Jewish friend, I contested it until I finally resolved the tensions by saying, "Jesus is love and we need to accept him as Christians, but we do not know what God does with people of other religions and we cannot say God does not save them in God's own way."

Shortly afterward, when my friend's father died unexpectedly, I felt a further, more urgent need for resolution. Although she did not seek my opinion on her father's salvation, I told myself, "Love is what is most important here. He lived a life of Love, and if that doesn't save a person, then nothing can save anyone." I mentally morphed John's verse into, "No one comes to God except through Love." So by then,

God's existence to me meant something about free will and living a life of Love.

Communities of Support and Pain

Throughout those late adolescent years, as I kicked at the ashes of my freshly ruined reality, hoping for new life to spark, several other faith issues left me without peace. I questioned the existence of God in light of my family's disintegration, the value of a religion that made life more difficult for some, and the authority of the church. Thankfully, the church I grew up in taught me about community during the sixteen years that it kept me under its wings. I remember more of the "joys and concerns" than I do the sermons, and I know that I felt a fondness for this church that was my primary social world. I owe that faith community much respect and much love for the support, the encouragement, and the strength it gave my family and me during those impressionable years.

But at the precarious age of sixteen, during my parents' divorce, my church taught me a new, painful lesson about community. My mother was "relieved" of her church responsibilities; she was told that in light of her failing marriage, she was simply dealing with too much. So at the age when I would have been exploring baptism, I was filled with rage instead, and I could not go to church. I have not been a steady member of a church community since.

Goshen College was the next setting for me to explore scriptural text, in both a religious and educational context. I found myself intimidated in the Biblical Literature class because I knew little about the Bible, and the Lancaster-area Mennonite kids could make me look foolish with their Bible skills. But I felt no obligation to know everything and simply enjoyed hearing the old stories in new ways. Biblical interpretation was a liberating concept for me, allowing me to relax knowing that the Bible is not to be read literally. Even the church, as a body of people, could misinterpret the profound text.

During my senior year I took a course with Shirley Showalter, then Goshen College president, which tackled the idea of the "Anabaptist Voice"—what it means to be an Anabaptist, or a Mennonite. As part of the course, we spoke with J. Lawrence Burkholder and Mary Eleanor Bender, who gave me the idea that people have a relationship with the church and its institutions. These conversations encouraged me to seek peace in my own conflicts with the church.

I took my faith and culture into my own hands and asked a group of women to share their journeys with the church, and I compiled their stories in a book as my senior project. Although I had to publish it myself, because Pinchpenny Press refused it (another point of contention and a question of "the text" and who edits it) those reflections and the experience of collecting them were moments of recognition and healing for me. These women struggled with the church and their faith, and some had chosen to cobble together a faith that fit them better; I realized I could do the same.

While my early religious education came from the church, my more recent theological education has come from engaging my community and from interacting with my English classes and my peers. At this stage, I am an English-major-theologian of sorts, seeing text—Scripture—in all places and peoples by considering the politics around them—what is published and held up and what is unheard or unspoken. My intention is not to be a universalist but to find that which is truly universal and ground myself there.

Yearning for a Faith Community, Yet Remaining on the Outside

After nearly a decade of pulling myself together again, I feel that my sense of faith and community is based on my Christian upbringing, but it is a way of being I constantly desire to articulate in a more universal sense. I can neither deny the feeling that there is deep connection running through all humankind nor deny the greatness of God by labeling "him" with one name. That is why, though the lifestyle I strive for fits with Jesus' teachings, I hesitate to embrace the name of "Christian."

What I have learned about the Christian church, and specifically the Mennonite church, is that not all people are accepted, despite Christ's message. The church often ostracizes and rejects rather than loves and supports those dealing with divorce, homosexuality, abortion. The church is human and imperfect. That is only natural, but it is frightening in the face of the church's claims to truth and authority.

I also recognize that the church is changing—what was unacceptable forty years ago is now commonplace, which suggests that what is unacceptable now may be permissible in the future. I am saddened to think of the pain and suffering the church causes those currently struggling with issues that may someday engender support rather than scorn. Specifically, I am crushed to see my gay friends pushed out of the church that nurtured them in their youth while others are simply silenced.

For me, these issues are not controversial; the way communities of faith handle these issues is crucial. I would rather wait forty years to join than suffer the painful debate now. Most important to me is people's basic approach to life: Do they try to live a life of Love? To me, this is the only measure that matters.

My ultimate struggle with the church is one of belonging, and I keep returning to the same question in different words: Do I fit here? If this tradition has formed me and shaped my ethics, but the church now denies my current lived experience, what shall I do? Shouldn't I strive to be an influence on the church as well? Invariably the answer that keeps returning to me in different forms has to do with the community immediately around me. The "church" as an entity is too enormous to confront. I have found a community that fits for me: former/under-the-radar, liberal Mennonites. The irony, perhaps, is that I still yearn so deeply to be included under the general label of Mennonite; while I celebrate finding connections with other religions, I grieve the separation I feel from my own.

One of the key things that saves me and keeps me relating to the Christian faith is 1 John 4:8b's affirmation that "God is love." This verse caught me before I could let the Bible go. God, to me, is the energy and possibility of Love in the world—a "life force" instead of a "personal being." I let my mantra be "God is Love." I insist that Love is greater than either the biblical text itself or Christianity. Only Love defies the chaos of the world we live in; Love lasts when we cannot.

Given that belief, my faith can easily fit into a Christian scriptural framework. Jesus lived a life of love, and Jesus' death shows us that love never dies. The story of Jesus' resurrection is valuable because it shows that when it seems like all hope has died, we have to resurrect love ourselves.

Jesus' death says, "Love is the only thing that matters in the end." The eternal life we have is the Love we have created and added to the universe, because that is the only thing that lives on. My heresy begins after this point, when I look to people like Gandhi and Mother Teresa, or even my aforementioned spiritual texts, who seem to offer the same message. The same "main point" of Christianity is found in every major religious tradition, I believe, so why would I pick one, or if I did, why insist it was ultimately the only way?

The challenge I face is that by reducing (or maximizing) God to being just Love and refusing to endorse a specific religion, I have no easy framework in which to ground my spiritual practices. My faith is largely unscripted, and this challenge invigorates me. I feel I retain the responsibility to serve God by not leaving the weight of the world for a mystical power to carry. I explore every way of glorifying the power of Love that connects us all, as I believe that this has the strength that can bear the load of us all.

In preschool, while coloring a picture of a hot air balloon, I learned the meaning of "infinity." I contemplated for the first time what it meant to go on forever, even if I was just imagining a hot air balloon flying up, up, and away into the vast universe. As I continue to live out my faith, I try to realize the immensity of Love and keep the perspective that this life is passing and only Love can be passed on.

Scripture to me is the collection of echoes of Love, in words, texts, and actions, as they resonate and return from all corners of the world. I heard the message in my own language and now listen beyond the limits of my tradition's language, trying to hear the message in every tongue. Only in the vastness of human experience can we find what is common and what is true, and only then can we appreciate the greatness of what God—what Love—really is.

CHAPTER 7

Wrestling
with a Perfect Jesus

Sarah Kehrberg

Like many people reading this, I suspect, I grew up with the Scriptures. The sixty-six books of the Old and New Testaments were my first storybook, then chapter book, then play, drama, comedy, tragedy, and musical. I could talk for quite some time about my journey with Scripture in general and various Scriptures in particular. Few mean the same to me today as they did when I was memorizing them in third grade.

In the first decade of my life, many a day ended with baths, nightgowns, and fighting over who would sit on top or on either side of Mom while the nightly story was read. In this way, Daniel and his lions crisscrossed in childhood fantasy with Aslan and the White Witch. Moses floated in his basket down the creek in the pony pasture, past Buster Bear's den and Reddy Fox's lair. Elijah was carried off in a fiery chariot and Peter Pan took Wendy, John, and Michael to Never-Never Land.

This is not to say I did not know the difference between the biblical truth and a passing secular yarn, but the world was alive with magic and make-believe, and the lines got fuzzy at times.

Learning the Basic Concepts

Sunday school each week helped to solidify the difference. This is where concepts were taught: God is love. Jesus loves me whether I am bad or good. Jesus died for me. God and Jesus care how I act—and I should act good. There were always verses that accompanied each of these lessons, but none stick with me. At home we memorized longer sections, like 1 Corinthians 13 and Psalm 121, and discussed their meaning. At Sunday school we mostly received stickers for attendance and learned social skills.

I would readily admit that the Bible was primarily a storybook for my first ten to twelve years of life. I heavily favored the Old Testament, with its wild characters; high emotions; outlandish behavior; and blood, guts, and gore. It was thrilling for the imagination, but even, and perhaps especially, as children we connect emotionally with the characters we meet. And I connected with these people.

The Old Testament is all about humans, rather pathetic ones most of the time, whom God chose and with whom God somehow worked. There is the dramatic character development of Joseph, who after being persecuted beyond measure comes around and offers complete forgiveness to his despicable brothers. The Dr. Jekyl/Mr. Hyde nature of David was always sobering. First he is the cocky little kid who slays the giant, then the victim who innocently flees the demented Saul and his hurling spears, yet spares Saul's life in the cave. But later David murders a man to steal his wife (whom he has already seduced or raped). Or consider poor Esau, who is too much of a brute to realize he is being cheated left and right, while slimy Jacob somehow ends up with everything.

These were characters who—we were told—were good; they were the fathers of our faith and even "after God's own heart," yet they did bad things. Somehow this worked. I remember my mother explaining that God uses fallen humans for his purposes, but I do not really remember being bothered by the question in the first place.

And then there was Jesus. I heard a lot of stories about Jesus and was coached to profess love and devotion to his name. But honestly, as a child I never felt anything but disbelief at his goodness, and maybe even pity for him. He was like that perfect, little girl in Sunday school who showed up each week with not a hair out of place, never slipped up on the memory verse, and wore a cute hat and matching dress with her mom to church on Easter Sunday. Here was perfection (for what truth was enforced more readily than the idea that Jesus did not sin?), and I could not relate. We were told that Jesus was "a friend next to ya" and we could scratch his back and pinch his cheek, but I never saw him. He never spoke to me as I understood speaking, not even in my heart. Besides, he was a middle-aged, bearded man who gave sermons and healed people. He was not my idea of a stellar playmate. Not that I did not like him or thought ill of him. He just was not as sympathetic a character as, say, Moses, who was tromping around the wilderness with a stuttering problem (I stuttered horribly as a child) and sometimes lost his temper and just banged the rock instead of "using words."

Trying to Understand Jesus

I spent much of middle school and high school feeling guilty because I had not had a conversion experience yet and did not seem to be getting any closer to having one. I went to a Christian high school and wrestled with the finer points of Paul's logic, Jesus' bizarre teachings, and my own need for salvation. I was baptized as a sixteen-year-old. I felt then and affirm today that it was a genuine experience. I pledged to walk in the newness of life and be a Christian to the best of my ability, and I am still doing that. But had I let Jesus into my heart? Was I saved?

I noted earlier that I could talk a long time about my various journeys with Scripture, but obviously, I will limit myself here. Yet if I have had a journey with Scripture that came to some kind of turning point, it has been my journey with Jesus and trying to understand and love him—which makes sense, Jesus being the author and perfecter of our faith and all.

There were and still are several hurdles to Jesus, for me. First, even accepting that he spoke in hyperbole and metaphor, he is really harsh. Like in Luke 9:57-62 when he does not let the poor kid go bury his father and admonishes him by saying, "'Let the dead bury their own dead; but as for you, go and proclaim the kingdom of God.'" Or Matthew 12:46-49, when he denies his own mother, the holy virgin Mary. Or Luke 11:50-51, where he says that "this generation may be charged with the blood of *all* the prophets that has been shed since the beginning of the world" (emphasis mine). And he liked to talk about "weeping and gnashing of teeth" plenty enough for me.

Having been raised an Anabaptist, I may be more comfortable than most with taking passages like "turn the other cheek" and "the first shall be last" seriously and literally. But with each new read-through of the Gospels, I find Jesus just as fanatical as the first time. In Matthew 18:7-9, he advises self-mutilation of the physical body to remain pure in spirit, then in the next chapter (Matt. 19:29) he predicts that those who have abandoned their families, including their children, for the kingdom's sake will be honored. You have to be nuts to follow this guy.

Maybe more troubling is the fact that no matter how literally or figuratively I read Jesus, or how much historical context I apply to the Scriptures, he is still confusing. What does it really mean that the kingdom of God is like yeast in bread dough (Matt. 13:31-35) or a seed that grows and is then harvested (Mark 4:26-29)? Why does the man without wedding clothes who comes to the banquet, with all the other riffraff from the highways and byways, get singled out so cruelly? Why is it that "many are called, but few are chosen" (Matt. 22:1-14)? What does pouring new wine into old wineskins have to do with fasting (Luke 5:36-39)? And the parable of the dishonest steward in Luke 16 is just plain backwards: Who is the hero here? What are we to learn from the story?

Then there is the book of John, where Jesus seems to spend most of his time explaining who he is in very convoluted ways. He generally goes on and on about "being from the Father" and "going back to the Father" and he does "all things through the Father" and the "Father does all things through the Son," and so on. The gospel writer says the Jews were divided and many said, "He is demon-possessed and raving mad. Why listen to him?" (John 10:20). With the theology of the Trinity several centuries from being articulated, I cannot say I blame them.

This is not to say that I ever really disbelieved. I am not that adventurous. But I am a fairly safe person, and honestly, I probably would not have liked Jesus, a man so obnoxiously insulting to every preconceived prejudice and cultural understanding. Just read the parables of the Good Samaritan (Luke 10:25) and the Prodigal Son (Luke 15:11-31)—beautiful as they are, they are shocking in his context. In general, he was so positive he had all the answers—the pearl worth an entire fortune, the one sheep worth the remaining ninety-nine. And . . . he never sinned.

Yes, Jesus had human skin, but he was God, after all. How could he be truly human if he knew he was the Son of God from his early teens (Luke 2:41-52)? More importantly, how could he be truly human if he never once screwed up?

The writer of Hebrews says, "For we do not have a high priest who is unable to sympathize with our weaknesses, but we have one who in every respect has been tested as we are, yet without sin" (4:15). But was he really tempted in every way, just as we are?

Life here on planet Earth is full of choices, literally millions we must make every day. And I am convinced that each one is a temptation. One wrong choice leads to a small sin like a judgmental thought or a big sin like adultery. As I have experienced it, the out-of-the-blue offer to work for an evil empire or sudden sexual come-on from the boss are not the temptations that bring people low; the day-to-day choices are what eventually defeat the average human.

When I read the Bible, Jesus did not experience this. He had one temptation experience in the desert that, granted, was intense—forty days with no food or drink and the devil in the flesh to do the tempting—but once he came out of that victorious, he was home free. Literally, in the gospel accounts, Jesus never once makes a nod at indecision except in the Garden of Gethsemane. He always has the right reply, quip, or action.

A Turning Point with Scripture

My turning point with Scripture was not about actual Scripture as much as how I read it, accepting what is and is not there. Once, in a typical college conversation about faith in which I was defending traditional Christianity, I happened to mention that at some point you need to be "saved." I am not sure why I used that terminology, because as I intimated earlier, I have never been a proponent of this theological jargon, never having been "saved" in that once-in-a-lifetime way myself. My conversational sparring partner burst out laughing and said, "Saved?! From what, Sarah, what do I need saved from?" It was a great question, and I am not sure where I got the answer but it came fast: "From yourself. From myself. I need saved from myself."

Since then I have come to understand that what I was articulating was that as a human, I need to be saved from my own choices, my pride, my desires—myself. Jesus was human and he needed to be "saved" from these, too. I do not read those feelings in the Scripture, but I believe it.

In my work with Herald Press I managed David Shenk's book *Journeys of the Muslim Nation and the Christian Church* (Herald Press, 2003). In summary, it is a comparison of two of the world's major religions, particularly in regard to their beliefs and mission. One significant difference between Islam and Christianity that I had not realized before is their approach to Scripture or revelation. Muslims believe that Mohammed, an illiterate peasant, was given the revelation of Allah and wrote it down. This is the Qur'an. It cannot be translated or changed in any way. Humans do not affect Scripture or revelation: it is sent down and set for all times.

Not so with Christianity. Humans had a large part in bringing together our Scriptures and we continue to translate, reinterpret, and decode their meaning. To Muslims this proves that our revelation has been tampered with and is therefore faulty. To Christians it shows how the Holy Spirit continues to work in the life of the church and the kingdom of God.

In this ever-changing spirit of our revelation, I propose a change to Scripture. I wish the temptation of Jesus had not been written as a single, monumental event. This encourages the idea that once you recognize your sin, reject the devil, and get saved, you are in the fold and safe from harm. This is not the experience of a human being. After baptism or conversion or that one particularly tempting time in the "desert," there is, sadly, plenty more to come.

I wish the writers of Matthew, Mark, Luke, and John would have included anecdotes of Jesus being confused about his ministry, being unsure what to do at times. I wish we could hear of his struggles to overcome his desire for a normal life with a wife and children and a comfortable bed to sleep in at night. I am sure he had to pray in earnest not to lose his temper and strike out at his stupid disciples, the fickle crowd, and the self-righteous Pharisees. And surely he was tempted many times to choose a different path than the one that lead to a criminal's cross. After all, Luke tells us that "when the devil had finished all this tempting, he left him until an opportune time" (4:13). The devil was around, he just is not mentioned.

But I will leave that improvement to those more qualified. Meanwhile, I read that Jesus prayed alone a lot—surely he was praying to God to save him from all those temptations. I am drawn to a savior who promises if we ask, "it will be given to you; seek and you will find; knock and the door will be opened to you" (Matt. 7:7). When a leper comes to Jesus and says, "Lord, if you are willing, you can make me clean," Jesus replies, "I am willing. Be clean" (Matt. 8:2-3). I may not fully understand it when Jesus says, "If any want to become my followers, let them deny themselves and take up their cross and follow me'" (Matt. 16:24), but I am challenged and content to try.

Jesus can still really get under my skin; he did claim that

> "I am the bread of life. Whoever comes to me will never be hungry, and whoever believes in me will never be thirsty. . . . This is indeed the will of my Father, that all who see the Son and believe in him may have eternal life; and I will raise them up on the last day." (John 6:35, 40)

This is a confession that I, for better or worse, have determined to hang my mortal soul upon. And I can sing, with sincerity, the song: "Give me Jesus, give me Jesus. You can have all this world, just give me Jesus."

CHAPTER 8

He Will Baptize You With the Holy Spirit and with Fire

Tasha Clemmer

My eighty-nine-year-old grandma still takes her hair down at night and kneels by her bed to pray. She believes in heaven and hell. When I showed her pictures of the January 2003 March on Washington, D.C. protesting U.S. involvement in Iraq, she shook her head, motioned to the ground, and said you have to pray to the Lord, it's in his hands. She said this because I asked her what she thought. She said she doesn't understand most of the news, "I'm like a sieve. It goes right through me." But she is certain about the Lord. She has her face turned toward heaven.

I don't pray to a God called Lord. I believe my morals are being checked by something greater than myself, but I don't think in terms of salvation. My actions don't come from a fear of hell or hope for heaven (though if there is a heaven, may I go). I nod in understanding when people talk about the Bible as Christianity's mythology. I think Jesus can serve as a role model for ethics. So can the Buddha. I am a product of urban, intellectual multiculturalism. I am not pagan or Wiccan, but I understand why they exist.

You ask about "my journey with Scripture" and I'll tell you I don't have one. Memory has a funny way of making it seem like what I know now has always been. But at the age of seventeen, I talked with my father about God and was shocked to discover that he did not unequivocally believe in heaven or hell—that he didn't think the Bible was necessarily a divinely inspired, literal documentation of history. The memory I have of this shock lets me know I once held different assumptions about Christianity.

So what about my journey?

In the World, But Not of the World

I was born being told, "You are Mennonite. God created the world in seven days. Eve ate an apple and got Adam to do the same. The Garden of Eden disappeared. Moses brought ten commandments (thou shall not kill).[1] And Jesus, God incarnate, is the example of how to be good (do unto others as you would have them to unto you).[2] There's a heaven. There's a hell. This is who you are, this is who we are. We live in Lancaster, Pennsylvania. We go to Community Mennonite Church of Lancaster. We don't believe in war. We're slightly different from other Americans."

Within this conformity I developed a sense of individuality. The uniqueness I felt came not from the Bible itself but from Mennonite critique of the U.S. government. I was the only kid in grade three who could not join the Brownies because my mom thought it was too patriotic. And the only one who sat during the Pledge of Allegiance to the flag.

Still, the Bible, through the example of Jesus Christ, had a definite effect on my emerging sense of right and wrong. I came home after a week at Camp Hebron, the summer before sixth grade, and told my sister I loved her like Jesus did. I had had a revelation during the fervor of camp songs that it did not matter if she was a jerk to me. I didn't have to be affected.

I took this idea of Jesus' love beyond the family. Riding the school bus that fall, I declared that I loved each kid in the class, adding "like Jesus does" at the end. I secretly hoped to challenge their notion that love only meant kissing and holding hands. Somehow I wanted to acknowledge a higher, more powerful love that made disagreements and unpopularity inconsequential. I was pointing to something that moved beyond the immediacy of "I like you," "I hate you," "Donald smells bad." Acting with a bigger idea of love felt new, different, and gave me a sense of power. I was sure of this new idea.

Leaving public school for Lancaster Mennonite High School (LMHS),[3] my unique Mennonite identity was replaced by a new kind of difference. Some of it resulted from how we interpreted the Bible. When my best friend told me that she expected her husband to be the head of the household because of a Bible verse, I felt sorry for her. Nor did I believe in biblical passages condemning homosexuality. This, too, was the time when I was becoming aware of not needing exclusively to use "he" for God.

I didn't use Bible verses to support my ethical and political views as some of my LMHS friends did, though I probably could have. And where the Bible seemed at odds with my opinions, personal experience took precedence. I didn't make the conscious decision to ignore problematic texts; it just felt clear that what I experienced as Truth was Truth. This clarity was fostered in the open-minded, inclusive church I grew up in, and my beliefs ended up reflecting this congregation's biases.

As a whole the Bible wasn't problematic because the stories were part of history, as real and relevant as other parts of history. You can ignore parts of history, but you can't dismiss it. Sometime during college at Conrad Grebel (in Waterloo, Ontario), however, my attitude toward the Bible changed from reverent ambivalence to disinterest.

I took several religious studies courses, including feminist theology, in which we read about women who were reconceptualizing the Bible by writing women back into the text, bringing existing women to the fore, and reinterpreting certain passages that were traditionally problematic in light of women's experience. I even went to an Anabaptist Women Doing Theology conference held in Winnipeg, Manitoba. During these investigations into Scripture, I was interested in—but not passionate about—the conversations at hand. The dialogue held particular value for the field of theology and for individual lives affected by new ways to approach the Bible, but I felt out of place, perhaps because I had never been burned by the text, as had some other women present. I didn't have to "re"-anything because I had never lost anything.

My last concerted effort at dealing with the Bible revolved around Jesus' gender. For the first time, I wondered if his decision-making process would have been possible or the same had he been female. I wondered if and how his status as a role model was weakened by his sex. Critiquing the nature of his message based on his maleness led me to consider it based on other factors like his social position in society and his economic standing. This was revolutionary for me because I had never asked questions of or about Jesus, the perfect of perfect, the way I scrutinized others who also served as ethical role models, such as Gandhi and Martin Luther King Jr. The connection between one's life and one's message became fundamental. Even Jesus needed to be critically evaluated to take his teaching seriously.

By the end of college, any intellectual curiosity I had had regarding Scripture faded, and I moved back to the United States to live in a city and experience the real world. The city became Washington, D.C., when the National Organization for Women (NOW) accepted me as an intern. During a trip to the Supreme Court, I had the distinct, physical sensation that I did not belong in that building—that I was somehow removed from its jurisdiction. This was a continuation of the unique feeling I had had in childhood that I, again, attribute to Mennonite identity rather than Scripture per se. In the months following, it occurred to me how off-base that feeling was because the structure of my life was based on rights mandated by laws created and interpreted in that very building and buildings like it. This realization was part of my entry into the world as one world, not two. I realized that feeling separate was preventing me from fully understanding my position in society.

In the City: Practical Applications of the Word

I'm getting older now. I've been living in New York City since April 1998. My initial whimsical flirtation with the city has morphed into the realization that this is my home. I'm making decisions that require one to not move for awhile. I've started attending church regularly for the first time in ten years. And I'm participating in a Bible study group for the first time in my life. Like the other decisions I have made regarding Scripture, this one feels less a choice than an extension of preexisting thoughts. My typical, pious, Mennonite concerns with fairness and Truth did not wane in the time I spent not going to church. If anything, they grew more acute. It is in this spirit of seeking transformation that I return to the text. Or, that the text has returned to me.

I find myself inadvertently thinking the "What would Jesus do?" question. I don't mean to—the question recalls something formulaic and naïve from when I had little life experience. But I think it now when I'm asked for money, when I see people talking to themselves, when I pass neighborhood drug dealers. And I mean it; I so wonder what Jesus would do that I have mental arguments with his ideal.

For example, what if the beggar on the train is asking for donations for a homeless organization, which I know to be untrue since it is illegal for businesses to solicit funds on the subway? The person is hustling the riders for his or her own profit, exuding hustler energy as they walk by. A tourist might be conned, or a Christian might give as Jesus asks, or somebody might not care and just give. But considering how I feel about overt lying, do I give? What if I conclude that the gift Jesus asks of me is to give the gift of no gift?

Answering the Jesus question proves more complicated now that I'm in situations that before were only story. Giving to the poor used to appear as something not worth disputing. Now it's an issue I don't think about so glibly. In thinking about Jesus when I meet "the least of these," his decision-making process becomes relevant and useful. He is no longer an abstract moral role model, even when I decide not to give. Jesus and Scripture then take on a practical role in making decisions.

I'm not suggesting that they provide sufficient answers for ethics, but that they can contribute to the discussion. Take two examples: non-violence, and the ethical relationship between work and success. I have given particular attention to these two issues since moving to the city. What can Scripture, or the example of Jesus in Scripture, say to each?

Rather accidentally, my introduction to capoeira in the fall of 2000 has given me much to consider regarding nonviolence. Capoeira is a game, a dance, and a fight. The exact origins are disputed, but there is general consensus that it was developed by African slaves brought to Brazil in the seventeenth century to work the sugar cane fields for European profit. Capoeira developed as a source of empowerment to the enslaved. It was played as a pastime, but it was also used for self-defense and to kill.

If you were to watch people playing capoeira, you would see a group of people sitting in a circle, singing and playing instruments. In the middle, there would be two people doing a series of handstands and cartwheels, kicks and escapes. It might be fast or slow, aggressive or playful. A good capoerista appears to be trustworthy and harmless. But in capoeira, a smile and nod are more often a sign of danger than friendship. Capoeira teaches you to be quietly suspicious and to excel at trickery to win.

Honing the skill of trickery feels like it goes against my Mennonite upbringing. How does being deceitful meet with keeping myself open and honest? Does knocking someone to the ground contradict turning the other cheek? Even the songs we sing include stories of violent liberation. How do they coincide with "love thy enemy as thyself?"[4]

Playing capoeira and thinking about its violent implications causes me to think more realistically about pacifism. Specifically, who decides to be a pacifist and who doesn't? As an adult, I have been uncomfortable with saying "I am a pacifist." Part of my unease comes from the way pacifism was just handed to me. As my sixty-five-year-old Jewish friend reminds me, "The world's not like Lancaster, Pennsylvania, Tasha—safe, where everyone's nice to each other. My introduction to politics at the age of five was the knowledge that a good part of the world wanted me dead."

There's something about a learned belief in pacifism that's equally as simple as a learned belief in militarism. Though Jesus' message of peace provided a base for pacifism, sources outside of the Bible must make it real. Training capoeira widens my understanding of why violence happens. The apparent contradictions between Mennonite pacifism and violent liberation continue to feel like an irreconcilable duality, but I hope something may eventually give way.

These apparent contradictions have made me reticent to discuss capoeira with Mennonites, to the point where I've intentionally not used words like *attack* when describing it. On a recent occasion where I was more forthright about the art, the Mennonite response surprised me. While no one addressed the question of capoeira's overt violence, they did offer insight into how "trickery" can be used for good. One person pointed out that many cultures have had to use trickery to survive—as a means to preserve identity.

Another reminded me about the story of Menno Simons (sixteenth-century Anabaptist reformer) being stopped by an official while driving a carriage. The man asked, "Is Menno *in* there?" and Menno truthfully yet deceptively responded, "No, he is not *in* there" for he was driving in the open air. Yet another person quoted the Scripture verse "Be wise as serpents and innocent as doves" (Matt. 10:16), indicating encouragement for deception from the Bible itself. These comments have shifted my thinking regarding how learning the skill of trickery in capoeira could be compatible with nonviolent peacemaking.

The ethical relationship between success and work also has been at the fore of my thinking as a result of my experiences with unfulfilling work, unemployment, and exposure to the work of deli owners, taxi drivers, brick masons, window washers, bathroom cleaners, and other means of employment that may appear undesirable. I'm not sure what Mennonites are saying about the distribution of labor, nor do I know how interpreting Scripture can help resolve this apparent disparity. To me, it's a simple math problem: There aren't enough jobs out there for everyone to do what they want. We're always in competition with each other. Competition is, by its nature, unfair. I do not see Mennonites banging down the doors of factories to get a job. I see us wanting jobs as teachers, non-profit administrators, social workers, pastors, academics—the "good" jobs, the "creative" jobs. What would Jesus say about this? Sell all you have and give to the poor? Take up your cross and follow me. Leave the dead to bury the dead?[5]

I don't mean to simplify the example of Jesus, nor do I mean to disrespect the power of myth and symbol. I don't ask the Bible to provide all of life's answers. Rather I'm trying to discern the possibilities for its use. The irony is that the myth I'm critiquing is the myth I've been shaped by. When something shapes your eyes so much that it becomes part of your eyes, how do you rightfully know what your eyes see? Because I've been raised in the biblical tradition, I am comfortable to go beyond it. Knowing this makes me question the quality of my comfort.

If you really want to test the authority I give Scripture, ask me if I would give Adam and Eve to a child.[6] If I would raise her to think of Matthew, Mark, Luke, and John as part of her history. I can very well say yes. It's the tradition I know. It's as simple and complex as "yes." Give her something to stir over for the next century.

At age sixteen I was baptized, by choice. I was dunked under water in a river because I wanted to be baptized like Jesus. In my brief speech to the congregation I said that I saw people in my church trying to live like Jesus, that I thought this was a good idea, and that I wanted to also. I didn't feel differently about myself before or after this, but I remember thinking hard about baptism, looking for signs telling me it was the right decision, wondering if I should do it, and specifically wondering how I should feel. I have yet to answer this question.

Notes

1. Paraphrased from Exod. 20:13 KJV.

2. Paraphrased from Matt. 7:12 KJV

3. Today Lancaster Mennonite High School is part of the larger, multi-campus Lancaster Mennonite School (LMS) system, which offers grades kindergarten-12. LMS uses the Lancaster Mennonite High School (LMHS) name to refer only to grades 9-12, offered at the Lancaster Campus.

4. Paraphrased from Matt. 5:43 KJV.

5. Paraphrased from Luke 12:33, Matt. 16:24b, and Luke 9:60, respectively.

6. Telling a story is in essence giving someone a mythology.

CHAPTER 9

"How Much Longer 'Til We Get There?"

Jessica King

My journey with Scripture feels a lot like a long, painful car ride with a relative I am supposed to know and with whom I should have a lot to talk about. Instead, we toss around a bunch of trivia; once in a great while we touch on something particularly illuminating, though conversation is still fleeting.

I am humbled by the breadth of exposure I have had to Scripture and the lack of depth that I find at this point in my journey. I do not know what has contributed to this. My adolescent and collegiate attention span? The distraction of boys in my Bible classes? My preoccupation with the social and the trendy? A whole bunch of white male Bible teachers and preachers? I only had a handful of female teachers and professors across the board, and none were in the Bible department.

But excuses aside, I will share a bit of my story.

The First Milepost

I am a product of Mennonite education from ninth grade at Lancaster Mennonite High School (LMHS) in Lancaster, Pennsylvania, through graduation from Eastern Mennonite University (EMU) in Harrisonburg, Virginia. I finished those eight years of schooling with a great cumulative knowledge of trivia. High school Bible quizzing helped this, and perhaps helped trained me to look for the obvious and quantifiable instead of the nuanced and implied—I mean, how do you buzz in on the lessons inherent in a parable? I had an average sense of the Social Gospel movement (way more than most non-Mennonites my age, though), and a pretty limited take on Mennonite history and theology.

I also left with wonderful and respectable examples of intellectually engaged professors who were living their faith in ways that captured my imagination for and loyalty to both Christ and the church. These professors talked about evil and imagination, taught dark Swedish films, assigned readings from Annie Dillard, introduced students to West African French literature written during independence and studied onsite and in context. They shared deeply from their wide breadth of experiences as humans and Christians. Some of them are friends to this day.

Milepost Twenty-Something

I came to Pittsburgh as a post-graduate to participate in Pittsburgh Urban Leadership Service Experience—also known as PULSE and part of Mennonite Urban Corps. This program places young adults, drawn largely from Mennonite college and university campuses, in year-long job assignments or internships at organizations focusing on peacemaking, community building, and the arts. It was founded by another Lancaster native, also an LMHS and EMU grad, a Pennsylvania Dutchy-speakin' home-boy who journeyed with Scripture to the city and stayed put.

This was huge for me! To see an example of someone who came from where I did and turned all of his Lancastrian inbred wackiness into something beautiful and prophetic for the city—*with* the city—was inspiring. Moreover, he was someone (ordained at that) who claimed the biblical truth that there is room for all of us at the table—artists, women, wine-drinkers, gays and lesbians, doubters, culture mavens, fashion idols, homeless, servants, rich, poor, leaders, bread-bakers . . . you name it.

That year, we spent a lot of time talking about Scripture in ways I had never heard it talked about before. Not that it was that far off my map of experience socially—but to realize that the Bible held such relevance, inspiration, and mystery (good mystery to be discussed, analyzed, thought about like a good novel, not just dismissible confusion) was profound. To have been a Bible quizzer all those years and only discover the power and potential in Scripture for the first time at age twenty-two was itself a kind of revelation.

My work that year was at the Thomas Merton Center—founded by Catholics during the Vietnam War—and I learned much about the potential for unity and power within faith-based work. Pax Christi, Mennonite Central Committee, Catholic Workers, Mennonite volunteers, and Ten Thousand Villages crossed through it all. My rural Mennonite roots intersected so completely with urban Irish-Catholic Pittsburghers on a common mission—faith-based peace work. This all felt so informed and supported by the scriptural explorations we were doing as a group that year in PULSE.

That winter, I attended a Fellowship of Reconciliation Peacemaker Training Institute—a somewhat faith-based two-week intensive seminar—where I made fast friends with a witch, people of color, lesbians, potheads, atheists, Southern Baptists, Bosnian refugees, and communitarian Catholic sisters living on an organic farm in northern New Jersey. And there was unity. There was healing. I met God among this hodgepodge of people!

In all, that year I became aware again of the truths in Scripture: grace and forgiveness, Christ's unity, striving toward the kingdom of God, toward God's beloved community, toward the common good. This engaged, lived faith looked so different than anything I had seen— and so removed from the homogeneity of the American suburb and the middle-upper-class way of life I was so used to.

Two passages from Scripture had a profound impact on me that year. First was the Tower of Babel (Gen. 11:1-9). Instead of understanding God's scattering of the peoples as a punishment for human achievement as I had always heard it, we interpreted this story as an example of God's intervention on our xenophobic tendencies—our racial and cultural supremacy desires. Scattering languages and cultures became an equalizing force. Second was the third commandment not to make graven images (Exod. 20:4)—again, a reminder from a dynamic and changing God to not take our ideas and images of God to be the end-all and be-all. God is greater than we can imagine!

These were liberating Scriptures, and I could see their principles being lived out in the city in front of my very eyes. The Old Testament laid the groundwork for the New Testament work of Jesus—welcoming the outcasts, the ones on the margins, the people of color, women, the poor, the weak. And I knew for the first time that being on the fringes is a good, creative place to be because establishments are often corrupt or corruptible. I also knew that, as a Christian, I wanted to seek that up-side-down kingdom where the powerless and those on the fringes were the ones Jesus loves most *and* the ones able to love others the most.

My urban experience was confirming all of this—my new, albeit very limited, awareness of the pain of people of color; the pain of many women in this patriarchal society and church; the oppression of gays and lesbians, of immigrants, of the poor. All of this created a picture of this kingdom thing that I wanted to be a part of. I realized that Mennonites, both past and present, knew something special about all this upside-down stuff. About justice. About community building. About respect for neighbors. About communicating. About living on and with the land. And that informed my reading of Scripture even more.

"Just Exactly Where Are We Going?"

My biggest challenge so far in my journey with Scripture is how to be a faithful Anabaptist-Mennonite Christian in the twenty-first century, urban world. We are members of an oversaturated, over-marketed, and overloaded generation whose choices outnumber our dreams. My temptation has been to embrace being Mennonite for the identity (or the implied identity since we are often pretty much like anyone else). That identity could be marked either by an implied righteousness revolving around social justice and pacifism in these days of war in Iraq—or by a loyalty to upholding the old ways of doing things by taking the barn-raising, communitarian approach to life by working hard with my hands and cultivating the physical place in which I live. As a white, "ethnic" Mennonite in North America, I do find life much more rewarding when I claim an identity other than that of the status quo. Survival as a distinct Christian community in our culture requires resisting the temptation of old patterns.

In the late 1990s, my friend Kendra Yoder and I dreamt up a project of interviewing Mennonite twenty-somethings from across the country using a narrative approach. We called our project "Stories from a Postmodern Mennonite Diaspora: Building a Bridge from Tradition to Tomorrow." We interviewed six people and had dreams of interviewing many more; publishing a book; going on tour. . . . We took our amazing, artistic, and prophetic display to the Mennonite churchwide assembly, St. Louis 99. We created a website. We printed full-color brochures. We worked to publicize our vision through the Mennonite General Board's office for "young adults" (ironically run by a fifty-something white man). We attended meetings, proposed a young adult component to the Constituency Leaders Council on the policy side of denominational re-structuring, and poised ourselves to publish, fund-raise, and get this project going.

But no one, it seemed, really cared—few people shared our passion and vision. Few people visited our booth, read our literature, or listened to our stories. Admittedly, as twenty-three-year-olds, we did not know how to push our project very well toward success, *but* we had a vision in-spired by the church—inspired by Scripture: "Don't let anyone look down on you because you are young, but set an example for the believers in speech, in life, in love, in faith, and in purity" (1 Tim. 4:12). We were the church's young: dreaming dreams, having visions, working toward the future of the church in a meaningful and holistic way.

"How About Letting Me Drive for Awhile?"

Something that has come up for me repeatedly on my journey is vi-sion and inspiration, largely for the church, connected to the church, and inspired by Scripture, community, and theology. My entire adult life, I have worked only in and for church-related organizations and agencies. Yet in most cases, even now, the Mennonite church has been skeptical, insular, and generally unreceptive to my ideas and those of many friends. But I have continued the dreaming work with others— and the latest is coming to fruition in some amazing ways.

With a group of other young, mostly Mennonite folk, I helped found an organization called the Union Project. We are restoring an old church building to provide gathering and working space for artists, community builders, and people of faith. It is many things at once: an urban real-estate project consisting of the restoration of an abandoned church in an innovative, volunteer-driven way that often resembles Mennonite and Amish barn-raisings; the nurturing of a group of young, diverse, urban leaders in a project that builds capacity for upstanding and sustainable community work; and a vehicle for connecting art and faith in new and, we hope, prophetic ways. Ironically, the most respon-sive folks are Episcopalians and Presbyterians of all stripes. Mennonites are often a harder sell.

My journey with Scripture is intrinsically tied to the life and culture of the church—the Mennonite church. I love this church, with its history, identity, theology, lived faith, humility, service, work, love, community. But for the majority of my adult life—for the ten years since I have left my home church—I have not meaningfully participated in a Mennonite congregation. I feel sometimes that I have received more welcome and inspiration at Episcopal, African Methodist Episcopal, Presbyterian, and nondenominational churches than I have from Mennonites in my city. I do not know what this means for my future, and it scares me. I realize more than ever that my journey with Scripture is empty without the counsel and relationship of other believers who want to journey together.

More recently my journey has been bringing me closer to two groups of young Presbyterians: Christian artists living community and faith as well as young suburbanites moving toward the city, cashing in their liberal arts educations, intentionally studying the Bible, and formally cultivating their goals (many inspired by their faith) in an organized group of twenty-somethings. I am expressing my faith and respecting others in new and profound ways. I am shelving my cynicism regarding "Bible studies" and yuppie Christians to see that the body of Christ sometimes wears suits and ties or capri pants and mules and not just cut-offs and Birkenstocks. And for the first time in my life, my sandals and I walk right into the circle and love those sitting around it not because of their familiarity or their proximity to me in the social scope of things but because of our common love for Christ and the church and our unabashed hope to bring forth the kingdom of God—right here and now.

Around the bend, I see a new future. I am tired of being the quiet in the land. I am tired of not knowing my history. I am wanting to share how it has shaped me in ways that I have not always appreciated. I am wanting Scripture to inform life instead of life informing Scripture. I am wanting to fight for my faith, shake it up, work harder to live it and love it. I am wanting to let go of my "spoiled-child-of-God" complex where I have been handed (and accepted) a theology I have blindly embraced rather than fought and struggled to own and to live out.

This awkward car ride with my once-distant relative is finally getting interesting—we have a lot to talk about, and a long way to go.

CHAPTER 10

A Literary Skeptic's Reading of the "Holy Text"

Kevin Maness

I want to begin by acknowledging that I am no theologian or biblical studies scholar. I took an Old Testament class and a New Testament class while I was a student at Eastern College (now University, in St. Davids, Pa.), and that was just enough to show me the vast universe of knowledge I would need to possess to read the Bible well. We are living in difficult times in this information age. With the amount of data available increasing exponentially every few years, it seems like expertise is becoming so specialized. How can an intelligent layperson really believe he or she is reading the Bible the way it needs to be read? Perhaps that helps to explain why my own journey with Scripture has become increasingly individualized and idiosyncratic as the years go by.

My journey with Scripture began like that of many children raised in the church. I learned Bible stories in Sunday school and in vacation Bible school during the summers, in children's sermons on Sunday mornings, and eventually in the "adult" service when I was old enough to stay. I learned the Old Testament stories of Adam and Eve, Cain and Abel, Noah, Abraham and Sarah, Isaac, Jacob and Esau, Joseph and his brothers, Moses and Aaron, the Ten Commandments, Samuel, Ruth, Saul, David and Jonathan, Solomon, Esther, and all the other Old Testament heroes and prophets, kings and queens, as well as the parables, stories, and miracles of Jesus as told in the New Testament. I never had to memorize much Scripture as a child, but I knew these stories, and every story taught a virtue, some element of "right living."

As I grew up, the Bible became increasingly mysterious. I discovered that there are verses and stories we never really talked about in Sunday school, like all the times when God told the Israelites to kill every man, woman, and child in a city, or the times when God took care of these massacres alone. I found that some passages are not really intended to be literal truths, like the creation story in Genesis, which does not jibe with the best scientific theories regarding the origins of life on the planet. I learned that even the most avid scriptural literalists do not believe that we need to follow every law laid down in Leviticus, like the rules about cutting one's facial hair, wearing mixed raiment, or eating unclean foods—but they still insist on holding fast to others, like the prohibitions against homosexuality. I was taught that the Bible is, after all, a cultural product, created for a specific people at a specific point in history, and that its lessons for us are ambiguous, to say the least, even though the Scriptures also contain what may be universal truths that stand up to the test of time and move easily across cultural boundaries.

Changing Notions of God

At about this same time, high school or early in college perhaps, I began to believe that there is no reason that God has to be a person. I mean, "he" certainly does not have to be a he at all, and there is no reason to think that God would need to be either a he or a she. What if God is not a person in any way? The concept of being created in God's image could mean any number of things, after all, and it is contained in one of the least literal passages in the Scriptures anyway. And in all my experience, I have never seen the hand or face of God, or heard God's voice, or felt God's touch in any corporeal manner.

What if all the personifications of God are just that, personifications—poetic devices, metaphors, designed to make God more imaginable for children and other literal-minded adherents of Judaism and Christianity? What if God is more like a spirit? Like the transcendent oversoul of the Transcendentalists, or the more immanent flow of life of the Taoists, or the inner light of the Quakers? What if God is a being or even a force not sentient in any way I can fathom? What would this mean for my relationship with God, something we often spoke of in my American Baptist upbringing? What would it mean for the nature of prayer? And what would it mean for the Scriptures?

I do not remember what, specifically, I was taught about the origins of the Bible as a child. I guess I grew up with the rather vague impression that the Bible was "God's Word," that somehow God had supervised its composition, that God had dictated the text to its various authors from Moses to Ezekiel, and from Paul to John. Later, I heard more sophisticated explanations of how God was specially present as the biblical canon was established and as various translations were prepared (although no one ever really convincingly explained how the King James Version managed to be filled with so many flat-out errors or why God would ever allow a literary abomination like that green, faux-leather-covered *Living Bible* to exist). But what if there is no person-God who guided the composition and collection processes with a wise and intentional hand?

As a literary scholar, I know a little about canons and how they come about. I know how the politics of race, gender, and class, not to mention the politics of ethics, morality, and religion, work to shape the bodies of literature we deem worthy of academic study.

As a teacher, I have seen the kind of anguished debate that goes on in a high school English department when teachers are trying to determine whether we should teach William Shakespeare's *Julius Caesar* or Zora Neale Hurston's *Their Eyes Were Watching God* to the tenth-graders this year. The motives that drive these discussions are innumerable, and in the end the decision that emerges may be wise, and it may be feasible—or not—but it results from a complex combination of petty motives and good intentions, of idealism and compromise, of what should be done and what can be done. It seems to me that the editing of the Bible would have been a similarly human process.

Furthermore, I have written lots of poetry, stories, and papers, some of which were crucial to me, but I have never felt that I was receiving dictation from the heavenly Author. Even now, when I am attempting to tell the story of my faith, I am unable to attribute any of these words to a divine voice, although I hope that I am somehow attuned to God and that this story somehow aligns with God's Holy Spirit. Was the experience of the biblical authors any different?

I do not deny that the Bible's composition might well have been assisted by divine will in some way, shape, or form, but in my experience with divinity, God does not seem to have any problem letting humans botch things. Why should the Bible be any different? It just makes sense to me to believe that the inspiration that fueled the writing of the biblical text and its formation into a canonical work was little different than the inspiration that led C. S. Lewis to write the *Chronicles of Narnia* or the inspiration that led Albert Camus to write *The Plague,* and when it comes right down to it, I have learned almost as much about God from these "worldly" texts as I have from the Bible.

Emerging Skepticism

I guess what it comes down to is a considerable degree of skepticism. I have learned skepticism from my own experience and from my knowledge of history. Throughout time, it seems that every warring faction claims to represent God's chosen people; they claim that God is uniquely on their side, even when they are talking about the same God worshiped by their enemies. How different is this from the claims in the Old Testament that Israel is God's chosen people and that it is God who commands the slaughter of enemy nations?

In our more recent history, I have seen religion used to justify slavery and segregation, and in my lifetime I have seen God and the Bible used to cast a moral glow over the wars and hypocrisies perpetrated by president after president. It is hard for me to believe that this kind of corruption is new, and it is easy for me to believe that the authors of our books of the Bible injected a strong dose of self-justifying mysticism into their narratives—just as today's leaders and activists scramble to claim divine authorization for their own acts of social and political ambition.

The skepticism does not end there, of course. I would like to know, for instance, why so many millions of people throughout the ages have adopted the mythical history of the Jewish people as their own personal religion, including millions and millions heavily steeped in anti-Semitism. Is it God or is it Constantine, or is it both, who is responsible for making the religion of Israel the religion of the Western world? Is it possible that some religion less open to imperialism is just as holy, or perhaps more so because it has taught its adherents to eschew violent conquest? Maybe we should be looking for our religion in the meekest of the world's citizens, rather than in the most powerful. Maybe a text that divides its time between nation-building and church-building is not the only or the best text on which to base one's personal spiritual journey.

So, I am skeptical. But at the end of the day, I still call this Bible my holy text. Why? Partly it is an accident of birth. I was born in the United States in 1970, into a family of Baptists. For better or for worse, the Judeo-Christian tradition is my tradition. The stories I learned in Sunday school, and especially the stories of Jesus Christ, still resonate for me, albeit it with considerable interference. I have great respect for the world's other religions and I have dabbled a bit in Eastern spiritual texts like the *Tao te Ching* and the *I Ching*, but it is unlikely that I will ever feel as comfortable in those texts as I do in the Bible, even though these Asian traditions have impacted my own faith considerably.

Foundations for Faith

You see, my faith, belief, and identity are built on a multifaceted foundation, consisting of my experience (both personal and indirect), my intellectual meanderings, the people in my life, and the texts that I have experienced—including the Bible, other religious texts, and the wider world of literature. Therefore, my reading of the Bible is shaped and influenced by all of these other factors, and all of these other factors are affected, to some degree, by my understanding of the Bible.

For instance, at the center of my faith and my identity is the conviction that God is love. When I went to college I very intentionally set about to strip my faith down to its essential core, and love is what I came up with. I see love in the teachings, life, and death of Jesus. Love is at the center of the greatest commandments: to love God and to love our neighbors as we love ourselves. So, this active, principled, sacrificial love is a biblical principle; it comes from the Bible, but then it also serves to determine my reading of the Bible.

If I believe that God is love, for example, then it is hard for me to believe God would truly sanction the murder of innocents, as God appears to do throughout the early Old Testament. This biblical principle also influences my perception of the larger world. If the Bible says that Jesus commands us to love our enemies, is it really possible for me to support our nation's military and foreign policies when they are based on the belief that enemies must be killed and that enemies are broadly defined as any people whose governments stand in the way of U.S. interests?

For me, the Bible is just one facet of my faith development, albeit a slightly privileged one. Since my reading of the Bible is heavily influenced by my relationships, my intellectual activities, my experience, and my reading of other texts, my Scripture reading is highly individualized. But even this idea has some precedent in my reading of history. In the Bible, Paul writes to the Philippians, "Work out your own salvation with fear and trembling; for it is God who is at work in you, enabling you both to will and to work for [God's] good pleasure" (Phil. 2:12-13). This passage actually reminds me of the conclusion to Voltaire's *Candide* (or perhaps *Candide* reminds me of the Scripture passage). After blindly following the philosophical advices of his tutor Pangloss, even when they lead repeatedly to misery and disaster, Candide finally comes to the conclusion that we must each cultivate our own garden.

These two passages reinforce my belief that my faith, and even my Scripture reading, are very much of my own construction. Actually, I think this is true for everyone. None of us can read the Bible without seeing it through the lenses of our own past experiences; we are all cultivating our own unique faith gardens. For example, I have spoken to so many Christians, especially women, who struggle greatly with the patriarchal language of the Scriptures. Gender is just one of the many lenses through which we all view the Bible, and there is nothing we can do to eliminate the tint that these lenses bring to our reading. The best we can do, I think, is to discover what lenses we use and the effect they have on our reading of the Word and of the world.[1] As Paul acknowledges, this process is fraught with fear and trembling, for there is considerable margin for error.

So, my journey with Scripture continues. This year, I decided to read the Bible in its entirety for the first time, and I am making pretty good progress. At the same time, I am not sure what I am accomplishing. Mainly, I am realizing that there is so much I simply do not know about how to read the Bible. And I am becoming increasingly convinced that much of this book only has meaning for me if I create that meaning in the act of reading it. I still believe that there is truth—important, life-changing, and fundamentally good truth—to be discovered in these pages. But I do not believe that this book is the only, or even the best, place for me to encounter and learn about God. My faith and my identity rely more heavily on my own reason, on my relationships with the people in my life, and the experiences I have as a human being trying to live life in relationship with the divine Spirit, whatever that may be.

Note

1. On this, see Paulo Freire, "The Importance of the Act of Reading," in *Literacy: Reading the Word and the World,* by Paulo Freire and Donaldo Macedo (New York: Bergin & Garvey, 1987) as well as Valerie Weaver-Zercher's response chapter in this text.

CHAPTER 11

Scriptural Threads in the Tapestry of Life

Buffy Garber

B ecause I have felt confident of God's love and presence even at times of questioning, my journey with Scripture has been a largely positive experience. As a young child I attended a Wesleyan church with my family. I have memories of Sunday school, vacation Bible school, and Christian Youth Crusaders that met on Thursday nights. In those settings I learned about Jesus and about God and about biblical characters from the Old and New Testaments. I learned that God loved me and that Jesus died for me. In most of these settings, we were supposed to memorize Bible verses, often for some sort of prize. Memorizing Scripture was related to "hiding it in our hearts," and I knew this was an important thing to do because learning more about God's Word meant learning more about God and about the way I wanted to live and behave.

Spending Time with the Text

Thanks to an assignment for one of my seminary classes, I had the opportunity to analyze these formative experiences. Each student worked at filling in a chart titled "The Unfolding Tapestry of My Life," with various columns, each with a different heading. As I filled in the column labeled "ways time was spent," I realized I had spent a considerable number of hours reading the Bible from the time I was about eight years old through my high school years. I had been taught that it was important to take time each day to be with God and that this certainly involved reading the Bible. In the early part of my growing up-years, I often read the Bible from front to back and then started over again. The Bible, in this case a lavender Precious Moments New King James Version with my full name engraved in gold on the front cover, was God's Word and was complete and utter truth.

In high school, I began attending a Presbyterian church because I liked their youth group and was disillusioned with the Wesleyan church's youth group, whose meetings were more like social events. With my new Presbyterian friends I sang songs, prayed, and studied the Bible. I was especially attracted to the Bible study because we often went through certain passages verse by verse. I had the feeling I was learning more about the Bible and also developing tools for Bible study; the experience prompted me even more to read the Bible on my own. At that point in my life, such a practice was nourishing for me.

In addition to becoming better acquainted with the Bible through Bible study, during this same period I had an unusual but significant experience with Scripture. I am sometimes hesitant to tell this story because some family members and friends who are skeptical about receiving direct words from the biblical text, or about any sort of emotional faith, are incredulous. My youth group took a mission trip to China. One of our outreach activities involved taking Bibles across the border from Hong Kong to mainland China for Chinese Christians who did not have easy access to Bibles. As a group, we made several of these trips; before each one, I would pray, asking God for safety and guidance. During one prayer, a voice in my head clearly spoke a biblical passage to me. It was not a passage I was familiar with, so I tried to keep praying. The voice continued to drone on, repeating the book of the Bible, the chapter, and the verse. Finally, I stopped praying, turned to my Bible, and looked up the reference.

That passage, Mark 6:6b-9, one of three synoptic gospel accounts of Jesus sending out the twelve disciples, says, "Then Jesus went around teaching from village to village. Calling the Twelve to him, he sent them out two by two and gave them authority over evil spirits. These were his instructions: 'Take nothing for the journey except a staff—no bread, no bag, no money in your belts. Wear sandals but not an extra tunic.'" The passage continues with Jesus' additional advice about the disciples' travels, and Mark concludes by commenting on the success of their mission.

As I read this passage to myself in my room in the Kowloon International Hotel, I was not sure what to do about or how to respond to this word from Scripture. The purpose of the trip was to carry Bibles across the border to other Christians; was God really telling me to take nothing along on my trip across the border? If this was the message, it did not make much sense to me. Yet I had difficulty denying the power in the way these verses had come to me while I was praying, and they did seem to be applicable to what was going on in my life that day.

I finally decided not to take the suitcases full of Bibles that I had taken on previous trips. Instead, I left my camera in the hotel room and filled my camera case with a few hymnals. This small case was all I took with me that day. Nothing significant or unusual happened during the crossing. But I have always wondered what would have happened had I taken a full load of Bibles. I do not know the answers to the questions that experience continues to raise for me, but I have never regretted listening to what I still feel was God, using God's Word to speak to me.

Challenging My Understandings

Another key event in my journey with Scripture took place during my years at Goshen College. How I even made it to Goshen is rather coincidental, or providential. Although I grew up a scant half-hour south of Goshen, Indiana, I knew little to nothing about the college located in that town. I knew, however, that one of my friends was planning on going there, so when I took the Scholastic Aptitude Test (SAT) I filled in the little code for Goshen College. Later that summer, I received a letter from Goshen College telling me that if I chose to attend, I would receive a scholarship based on my SAT scores. Since I did not know what else I was going to do in the fall, I decided to give the school a try. While my knowledge of Mennonites was limited to recognizing them as members of another Christian denomination, I learned a lot from my Mennonite professors and classmates that has changed the way I view Scripture.

One of the first classes I took at Goshen College was Biblical Literature with Don Blosser. While I do not remember all of the specifics of the class itself, since it was nearly a decade ago, I do remember how frustrated it made me feel at times. I think part of the reason I no longer remember specific flashpoints is that issues that raised my hackles my first semester of college would not even make me raise an eyebrow today.

There were some very memorable moments, however. For example, I remember one class session about Jonah and his journey to Nineveh resulting in finding himself in the belly of a great fish. During the lecture, the professor made an astonishing claim: Jonah's story is a parable. This did not sit well with me! If we believed that Jonah was a parable, this somehow made the Bible less true, and the truth of the Bible was crucial to me. But the more I considered the perspective that our teacher shared with us, the more I began to realize that some parts of the Bible do not have to be historical facts to be full of truth. This lesson opened a new path for me along my journey with Scripture.

During those years at Goshen College, when my understanding of Scripture was changing, I also spent three summers working at Trail's End Ranch, a non-denominational evangelical camp in the southeastern corner of Montana. As I was being exposed to some Mennonite perspectives on the Bible at Goshen College, during the summers I was also asking questions about other views of Scripture because the people who ran Trail's End Ranch held a view of the Bible that stood in stark contrast to that of many of my friends and teachers back at college. However, these summers were full of meaningful experiences and important life-lessons. For example, at the camp, the King James Bible was the version of choice. Any other version, including the New International Version, was considered a paraphrase rather than a translation. This struck me as a little ridiculous at the time. And today, I would say with certainty and personal clarity that the King James Version is not any holier or more sanctioned by God than other translations.

Mulling Over the Questions

As I think about where I am in my journey with Scripture, one question rises above the others: What significance is there to the fact that I read my Bible much more as a teenager and high school student than I do now as young adult and seminary student? This does not feel like a good change to me. Though many things have changed about the way I view Scripture, God, and my own faith, I still see spending time reading the Bible as an important part of the Christian life. I continue to think about this, mulling over this question, looking for some kind of answer.

There are other questions I find myself wondering about. What makes the Bible holy anyway—what makes it holier than all the other literature also available to those in power who sat around millennia ago forming the canon? How and why is this collection of books holier than the wisdom, guidance, instruction, and inspiration we can sometimes receive from other sources?

What about the profound inspiration prompted by telling others in a small group our stories of faith? Or what about the insights we receive from a friend's letter, the poignant lyrics of a song, a powerful dream, or the simple beauty in a mother duck with her six ducklings trailing behind her? Is it less important to treasure these words, sounds, sights, and experiences than to treasure the words of Scripture? If I jot down a quote by a writer like Anne Lamott or a profound point made by one of my teachers and post it on our bathroom mirror, can I value it as much as I do Psalm 52:8—"But I am like an olive tree flourishing in the house of God; I trust in God's unfailing love for ever and ever"—a verse I have been appreciating lately? Should I?

How much flexibility can we allow ourselves as we question the Bible's authority? How many of its teachings can we let go of because they only applied to the culture of that day? How much do we need to say, "No, what the Bible has to say to God's people then applies to us as well?" Are there not some absolutes? Or can we live without such certainty?

There are many things I wonder about and question when it comes to understanding what Scripture is to me. Some of these things I am actively trying to figure out and others I have let rest for the time being. This is an okay place to be for me right now—questioning, wondering, thinking, and, as the psalmist says, "trust[ing] in God's unfailing love" (Psalm 52:8b).

CHAPTER 12

Wrestling with the Book of the Unexpected

Krista Dutt

The most rebellious thing I ever did in junior high school was read the Bible. I had heard that the Song of Solomon was about sex, so one night, I borrowed a flashlight from the pantry, grabbed my Bible, got into bed, pulled the covers over my head and turned on the flashlight and read . . . and did not comprehend one word of the supposedly sexual book.

The Bible represents a childhood faith for me, yet this book also has allowed me to grow within its pages as an adult. I still may not understand every lesson contained in its stories, but I can learn important principles like I did that night beneath the covers: what I expect to be there is not always there, but there is still a wealth of material in this book that helps us grow as people of faith.

Growing Up with the Bible

I was one of those kids who took her Bible to school, not because I actually read it there, but because I had a sense that it was an important thing to keep with me. I grew up in a family that went to Sunday school every week, talked about our lessons over dinner, and had a family night activity that would reinforce those principles. So when I became a student at Bluffton College (now University) in Bluffton, Ohio, I happily took the general education course Introduction to Biblical Literature.

How hard could it be for someone who had been reading the Bible most of her life to do well in this class?

Instead of being delightfully easy, the class made me mad. However, instead of getting angry at the professor as some of my peers did, I turned against my Sunday school teachers whom I loved, my parents who had encouraged me to trust what the Bible stories said, and anyone else I thought had lied to me. I was mad that I never learned the *real* stories in the Bible—the "bad" parts of the good stories or even the ways upstanding characters had been deceitful or manipulated others. Why, for example, had I not been taught about the episode in Genesis 12:10-20 when Abram tried to pass Sarai off as his sister, causing more hardship in Egypt? Throughout the term, I kept asking new questions about the cleaned-up Bible stories I had been told as a child.

I was energized by the new things I was learning. Instead of challenging or rebelling against the Bible, I enjoyed being challenged *by* it. I jumped into the hard texts with gusto, turning to the ones I did not hear or study in my Sunday school days. As in my experience in Introduction to Biblical Literature, the following six biblical wrestling matches with the Bible have led to unexpected learnings.

Match 1: I Am Woman and So Are People in the Bible

My experience learning about women in the Bible has been hard, yet life-giving. A second Bible course I took at Bluffton was titled Women of the Old Testament. Over lunch one day, my father and I started talking about my classes including Women of the Old Testament. He asked me, "How do you find things to talk about in that class? There are not that many women in the Bible, are there?"

Fortunately, it was a question rather than a statement, and I answered emphatically, "Dad, come on!" He insisted that his question was serious and proceeded to name the women in both testaments on two hands and several toes. I realized my father, who reads the Bible regularly, had a narrow perspective on the story of *all* of God's people. I also realized that my father's experience was all too common among people in the church.

This class challenged some of my assumptions and helped me realize that many women and men have not been given the chance to see biblical women in their contexts. The women my classmates had read or heard about were characters I considered harmful to women's self-image rather than examples of liberation and freeing passion for a God who loves the oppressed. This was the God I was looking for in Scripture and the God I found in places like Hagar's story in Genesis 16:1-15.

It was in Women of the Old Testament that I first met Tamar, whose story is found in Genesis 38. It might seem odd, but I find Tamar inspiring. In her context, Tamar had little to no rights as a woman. As a widow twice over, without children, who was unjustly dismissed by her father-in-law Judah, Tamar took her fate into her own hands. As the story unfolds, Tamar exacts justice for herself from Judah by posing as a prostitute.

Reading her story, I came to the conclusion that Tamar did nothing wrong other than to demand what was rightfully hers: a child by Judah's family. She is an example of what it sometimes takes to be an advocate for justice. There is a great deal of power in the way she made the decision to fight for her place in the community rather than remain powerless out on the fringes. Women of the Old Testament allowed me to cautiously step into the world of feminist theology and biblical criticism, preparing me for my next struggle.

Match 2: Bible, Schmible

After graduating from Bluffton, I attended Associated Mennonite Biblical Seminary (AMBS) in Elkhart, Indiana. Needing a change of pace from life in suburban Elkhart, I spent a semester in an urban seminary education program based in Chicago, Illinois. I was able to take a class at Loyola University, where I found my own way to relate to the hard passages of Scripture that often had to do with women.

One week we read the story of Abraham, Sarah, and Hagar. In response to the story my professor exclaimed, "I have a very hard time studying a book or truly agreeing with a church that allows the mistreatment of women." I agreed with her. The Bible does have too many stories about mistreated women, and I agreed that Hagar was mistreated.

Nevertheless, I believe the Bible is worth struggling through and studying, so I disagreed with my professor's conclusions. "But wait!" I said, "Hagar was the first to give God a name, she felt God's presence, and she had a male author telling her story—which means it is more likely to be true, since males at that time would not have wanted to give a female the right to name God. Hagar's story ends with hope, not hate."

My professor did not agree with me. The more I thought about it, the more I realized that while the Bible has stories I find terribly disturbing—accounts of rape (Gen. 19:1-10; Judges 19:1-30; 2 Sam. 13:1-20), Queen Vashti's dismissal from the court by her husband King Ahasuerus (Esther 1:10-2:4), or Paul's contradictory words about women's roles in the church—I still feel Scripture makes the basic affirmation that God's love is liberating.

Match 3: But Mom and Dad Cannot Be All That Evil for Having Money

Through an intensive book study of Luke's gospel in another seminary class and a small dose of inner-city living, the Bible challenged me once again. Before these two experiences, I had never thought about money being evil. In theory, I knew that money should not be deified and revered as a god. However, once I finished the Luke study and was reflecting on my first experience in the inner city, I believed without a doubt that money could be very evil. Money that was abused or otherwise misused in the suburbs was responsible for the ongoing destruction of my beloved South Side Chicago neighborhood. These lessons inspired and influenced me to take Jesus' teaching more seriously.

Growing up in a mainline Christian denomination, I thought about money and wealth very differently than most Mennonites I know. At least in my midwestern United Church of Christ congregation, we pretty much ignored the passages on money—probably because we had too much of it. After coming to the conclusion that following Jesus meant seeking *shalom* for all, I could not ignore any biblical passage about money simply because it might hurt my lifestyle. Rather, these tough passages call us to consider making sacrifices so that others might survive. Giving up a fancy car, a great paying job, or even my favorite Sour Patch Kids candy suddenly became an avenue to serve others and God because my choices were rooted in the principles of shalom.

Match 4: Peace in the 'Hood?

During the development of my shalom thinking, I had another inner-city experience that forced me to think about the limitations of my reading of the Bible to date. I was observing a Bible study for teenagers on Chicago's South Side. The group had been working through the Sermon on the Mount and the passage for the evening was Matthew 5:38-42.

The community where we were based had acquired a reputation for being a violent neighborhood, and that stereotype had already taken hold in the hearts and minds of these youth. The young women and men sitting together that evening were having a hard time understanding the purpose of nonviolence: Why, when confronted with violence, should they even consider not fighting back? In this context, *I* was having trouble understanding the rationale for nonviolence, and I was the pacifist in the group! In a neighborhood where children see fights breaking out numerous times each day, how should or even could we, together, understand a message to not strike back?

This experience of not knowing how to respond other than use the once-popular "What would Jesus do?" (WWJD)—and then be labeled a white elitist—sent me back to passages in Scripture that gave me grounds for my peace witness. I came out of that experience still believing that pacifism is God's way, but not sure how to apply it as a white person in an African-American neighborhood without violating *shalom* in other ways. The Bible raises this tension and yet helps me live with the tension.

Match 5: Love and Maturity

On September 11, 2001, I picked my topic for a semester-long project in my class Greek Three: Sermon on the Mount. I would work on Matthew 5:43-48, which begins with the familiar words, "You have heard that it was said, 'You shall love your neighbor and hate your enemy.' But I say to you, Love your enemies and pray for those who persecute you, so that you may be children of your Father in heaven; for he makes his sun rise on the evil and on the good, and sends rain on the righteous and on the unrighteous."

Because of the global crisis we found ourselves in, this assignment turned out to be an amazing spiritual discipline for me. I constantly looked at the statement "love your enemies" and asked myself who my "enemies" were. Were they the September 11 hijackers, the non-pacifists like my parents who felt the "war on terror" was justified, or the Mennonites who could not understand how lucky they were to have families who understood their peace position? While challenging me, this piece of Scripture also became immensely comforting, because I knew I was not alone in my struggle to live out the words of this text.

But loving my enemies was not the only lesson I learned during that class. I found that I also had become fearful of being mature. I learned very early in my study that in Greek, Matthew 5:48 reads "Be mature, therefore, as your Father in heaven is mature" instead of "Be perfect, therefore, as your heavenly Father is perfect." All my life I had written this verse off as some way to make us humans feel unworthy of God's love by a mean-spirited author; we human beings cannot be perfect. But now, I had to admit that it was possible for me to be mature—and that scared me! The last line of the paper I wrote for that Greek Three project probably sounded silly: "I want to be mature." However, for me this was a way of signifying my commitment to this wonderful passage and to all of Scripture in which I find strength and courage, wisdom, and power.

Match 6: The Importance of a Back and a Bible

After graduating from AMBS, I decided it was time to relieve my body of the back pain I had suffered for two years. This decision meant intense back surgery. While my friends were moving on to new adventures, I was stuck at my parents' home lounging while I healed. I was not living the life I expected.

I had turned down several job opportunities to have the surgery, and once I was able to look for a job, no one wanted to hire me. I needed some answers from God. Was I to live in small-town USA with my parents for the rest of my life? *I would rather die*, I thought.

Then one day, unexpectedly, a friend shared her favorite verse from Psalm 139 with me: "For it was you who formed my inward parts; you knit me together in my mother's womb. I praise you, for I am fearfully and wonderfully made." This was a hard passage to hear and digest. To deny that I had purpose *even if I could not see it* was, in fact, denying God's handiwork in creating and shaping my life, including the lack of pain I now felt because of the surgery. Psalms are not usually wrestled with, but I fought bitterly against the proclamation in this psalm. I had purpose just because I was God's child. Nothing else gave me such worth. This was a big lesson for a person who has usually defined herself by grades, extracurricular activities, and all-around productivity.

Always a Challenge

So I have circled the mat struggling to keep a tight grip on the Bible and at the same time resisting being overcome and pinned by it. Like any athlete, I have had a coach who helps me train for these matches. Mary Schertz, my professor and advisor at AMBS, has an ongoing dialogue with Scripture that includes gracefully taking on challenges. The way she does this has been life-giving and inspiring to me as her student. My wrestling match with the Bible is far from over. The Bible is something that continues to make unexpected moves, challenging me to think about myself and the world. I have to be prepared for these moves—but also learn to from them when they turn my world upside-down.

CHAPTER 13

My Journey With Sacred Texts, or How Mennonite Literature Changed My Life

Daniel Shank Cruz

My journey with sacred texts[1] has been a winding and enriching one, though not especially orthodox, at least when compared with those of my Swiss-German Mennonite ancestors. Mennonites have traditionally been a People of the Book. They have believed that some collections of words are powerful to the point of revealing the divine. I, too, have adopted this belief in the power of words, their ability to be Godde-revealing and life shaping.[2] I believe, and have since high school, that sacred texts are the pinnacle of the knowledge that we receive via language, that sacred texts are the best of the best and thus the most important words. As Maryland's poet laureate Michael Collier notes, "People have a deep need for encounters with language that exceed their normal daily encounters."[3] Sacred texts provide these encounters for us.

While this belief in the special import of sacred texts has remained constant since high school, the texts that I have viewed as "sacred" have not. The purpose of this essay is to give a short history of my relationship to these various sacred texts. I will present this history chronologically and then briefly examine two of my current sacred texts, Rudy Wiebe's novel *The Blue Mountains of China* and Jeff Gundy's "The Cookie Poem,"[4] to illustrate the role of sacred texts in my spiritual life.

The Good Guys Always Win

My earliest encounters with the Bible took place via an illustrated book of Bible stories for children given to my family by Jehovah's Witnesses when I was around three years old. My mother read from it often, and many of its illustrations are still etched quite vividly in my memory, especially the one depicting the drowning of the Egyptian army in the Red Sea. My favorite stories were the violent, action-packed ones from the Old Testament—David defeating Goliath, Samson getting his hair cut but later getting his revenge against the Philistines (I spent much time as a child hating the Philistines—they were the quintessential villains, arrogant and morally depraved), Daniel being delivered from the lion's den. The stories of Jesus' miracles were boring in comparison.

When I later discovered that it was possible to buy a New Testament without the Old Testament, but not vice-versa, I was dismayed. I now understand why this is the case, though I still enjoy Old Testament stories much more than New Testament ones because apart from being exciting they were also comforting: The good guys always won. I assumed these victories were a biblical norm and thus the way life worked in general, since even at that early age I had some sense that Bible stories were different from the ones in books from the public library—that they were somehow more special because Godde was involved. I knew that as Mennonites the Bible was our most important book. I also took Bible stories to be absolute historical truth, whereas library books, while sometimes being just as enjoyable as Bible stories, were not "real."

My next encounter with the biblical narrative was actually with a non-biblical text. This encounter began in first grade when my mother read me *The Lion, the Witch, and the Wardrobe*, the first book of C. S. Lewis' seven-part *Chronicles of Narnia*. I recognized it as a retelling of the story of Jesus: Narnia is held captive by the evil White Witch, but the great lion Aslan sacrifices himself to redeem the fallen Edmund and is then resurrected by a deep magic unknown to the White Witch to lead the forces of good to victory. This happy ending helped reinforce my assumption that the Bible was a happy book in which the good guys (and once in a while a good girl like Deborah or Rebekah) always won because Godde was on their side. At the time I had read nothing that indicated otherwise.

It was also during this time that I learned to read, which was a wonderful, freeing experience. I began reading anything I could get my hands on and purchasing books with my allowance. Being able to read by myself allowed me to experience books in a new way—*I* was the one holding the book, *I* was the one turning its pages, *I* was the one observing the harmonies between ink and paper. Interacting with stories became not only an emotional enterprise, but a physical one as well. Reading books became a full aesthetic experience that was enjoyable and addictive. Throughout my elementary school years, my addiction to books grew, and even though I had very little interaction with the Bible during this time my book addiction helped foster the notion that reading could be enjoyable in some sort of spiritual, soul-feeding way. I learned that books could touch me in deep places, a learning that would be essential later in my life.

During fifth grade my parents bought me my first real Bible, a New International Version. This Bible was bought during one of our frequent visits to Lancaster, Pennsylvania, at the Provident Bookstore (a bookstore chain until recently owned by Mennonite Publishing House, long a Mennonite denominational publisher). I loved our visits to Provident, which at the time was the largest bookstore I had ever seen. The aesthetic experiences of these visits played a major role in shaping my love of books. I decided to read through the entire NIV text—but lost interest almost immediately after beginning Leviticus.

This failed attempt was my last interaction with the Bible until eighth grade, when I attended a small Lutheran school, St. Mark's. At St. Mark's I had my first religion class, which consisted mostly of learning the Lutheran catechism and memorizing the order of the books of the Bible with a few Bible verse memorization assignments thrown in for good measure. The only concrete memory concerning the Bible I have from my year at St. Mark's is being yelled at by the principal for setting my Bible on the floor. This zealousness for the physical Bible struck me as horribly idolatrous.

Revisions and Transformations

I graduated from St. Mark's in June 1994, and a few weeks later my family moved from New York to Lancaster, Pennsylvania, where I began attending Lancaster Mennonite High School (LMHS).[5] It was at LMHS that the Bible came alive to me in a powerful way. The first-year Bible class, Creation and Promise, focused on the Old Testament and was taught by Glenn Sauder, a recent graduate of Eastern Mennonite Seminary. Mr. Sauder's seemingly magical knowledge of the Bible astounded me. I had always assumed that the only way to read the Bible was to take its stories at face value as literal truth, but he taught that many parts of the Bible, such as the first part of Genesis, were probably not factually true; rather they were regarded as myths by many who studied the Bible. I was initially scandalized by this idea but became more and more excited about it as the semester wore on. Mr. Sauder also knew Hebrew and would point out what he thought were mistranslations in the English text.[6] This concept that the biblical text we had in front of us was somehow fallible was also completely new and shocking to me.

Along with teaching us these new ways of viewing the biblical text, Mr. Sauder possessed a contagious enthusiasm for the Bible. One could tell that he thought the Bible was *incredibly cool*, and he himself was cool, so if he thought the Bible was cool it was definitely cool. It was this enthusiasm that caused me to begin thinking about studying the Bible in a concentrated way; I began considering attending seminary in the future.

However, after Creation and Promise ended, my interest in the Bible waned. My sophomore Bible class, Jesus and the Gospels, was taught by a less gifted teacher and did not capture my imagination at all. So I was once again at a place where I believed the Bible was somehow important for my spirituality, but I was unable to connect this importance to my everyday life.

This disconnect continued until midway through my junior year, when I underwent a conversion experience in which Jesus Christ made himself emphatically real to me. That experience happened on December 26, 1996. I was in the car with my family on the way to Harrisonburg, Virginia, to visit my grandparents, and I was listening to "Radio Song," the first song on R.E.M.'s *Out of Time* album, when I realized that Jesus would not listen to such music because it contained profanity ("I tried to sing along / but damn that radio song"). It was a true "What would Jesus do?" moment, and things snowballed from there.

The experience prompted me to reevaluate *everything* about my spirituality, including my relationship with the Bible. I began a second attempt at reading the Bible straight through and was successful. I read through it three or four more times during the next few years, believing it was the Word of God—the prescription for how to live a Christlike life. The Bible became my source for answers to all questions. The enthusiasm I had felt for it during Creation and Promise returned, and I decided during the early part of my senior year that I would major in Bible and religion when I enrolled at Goshen College the next fall.

During this period I also began reading books on theology and spirituality. This reading included texts by C. S. Lewis, Oswald Chambers, and Thomas Merton.[7] I also struggled through *The Politics of Jesus*[8] for the first time.

It was during this last year-and-a-half of high school that I discovered how unpleasant the Bible actually is. In my childhood all of the rapes, disembowelments, and other such happenings had been censored, so it was quite a shock to have to rethink my long-held misconception of the Bible as a happy series of miracles and resurrections. These new discoveries helped lay the groundwork for the gradual erosion of my reverence for the Bible during college.

My first year of college, beginning in 1998, was rather uneventful as far as the Bible was concerned, with only the introductory Biblical Literature class. I also co-led a small group Bible study with a good friend and fellow LMHS alumnus, with whom I had had many formative theological conversations during the latter half of high school.

In the fall semester of my second year I enrolled in a class titled Feminist Theology, and it was during this class that my view of the Bible began to change. We were introduced to the world of feminist hermeneutics, a world that often views the Bible as a text that is oppressive to women and thus must either be reinterpreted and reclaimed in a liberating way or disregarded altogether. I was intensely fascinated by these new ways of viewing the Bible. At that time I quickly discarded the views of radical feminist theologians like Mary Daly but was drawn to much of what more moderate writers like Elisabeth Schüssler Fiorenza and Rosemary Radford Ruether had to say. I was especially impacted by Phyllis Trible's *Texts of Terror*,[9] which approached stories like that of the Levite's concubine in Judges 19 with a feminist viewpoint to show the terrifying misogyny of the stories.

The way Trible and others dissected the Bible and reassembled it into something completely different, something oppressive, was tremendously exciting to me on an academic level. I still viewed the Bible as Godde-inspired and prescriptive, but had come to realize that, like other literary texts, the Bible was not untouchable—it could be manipulated and critiqued in what were possibly quite meaningful ways.

Discovering Mennonite Identity

Along with encountering these new approaches to the Bible at Goshen, I was also beginning to discover my identity as a Swiss-German Mennonite. This process of discovering my Mennonite self was sparked by a lecture given by Julia Kasdorf during the spring semester of my first year,[10] and continued in a concentrated way in the spring semester of my second year in three of my courses: Mennonite History in America; Religion and the Political Order; and War, Peace, and Nonresistance. In these classes I learned about influential Mennonite theologians of the past and present like Daniel Kauffman, Harold S. Bender,[11] Guy F. Hershberger, J. Lawrence Burkholder, and John Howard Yoder. During this semester I also took Liberation Theologies. There I encountered more feminist theology as well as Black theology and Latin American liberation theology.

I was strongly attracted to both types of theology, the Mennonite type because it seemed to tell my story and the liberation type because it seemed incredibly relevant to everyday life.[12] As the semester wore on, I read as much as I could in these two theological veins and continued to do so during my junior year. More and more I found myself looking to Mennonite theology for intellectual stimulation, but looking to liberation theology for theological truths.

During the second semester of my junior year, I had another conversion experience, one in which Jesus was not involved at all. I took Ervin Beck's Mennonite Literature course and was exposed to texts that moved me in ways I had not been moved before. The prose of David Bergen and Rudy Wiebe, and especially the poetry of Jeff Gundy, Di Brandt, David Waltner-Toews, and Julia Kasdorf, as well as Gundy's essay "In Praise of the Lurkers (Who Come Out to Speak)" all *totally blew me away*.[13] These writers were ethnic Mennonites struggling between the lure of the world and the safety of the faith community, and one result of this struggle was their writing, which I found to be supremely prophetic.

Their writing helped me get to a part of my Mennonite identity that had not been previously illumined by theology. This prophesying recognized that *Godde could be found in the world outside the official faith community* and that close-minded Mennonite separation from the world was quite possibly causing Mennonites to miss a significant part of the way Godde was attempting to move throughout humanity.

Reading Mennonite authors was like coming home; it was so liberating! These writers instantly became my idols—I wanted (and still want) to be like them more than almost anything in the world. I began writing my own poetry and reading as much Mennonite literature as I could find. It was at this time that I started understanding how it might be possible to have sacred texts other than the Bible.

In the fall semester of my senior year of college, I took Spiritual Writings of Women. After taking Feminist Theology two years before, I had continued to read feminist theology but only experienced the insights from this reading on an academic level. In Spiritual Writings of Women, feminist theology came alive for me in a practical way. It finally clicked that institutional Christianity was really oppressive to a lot of women, including some of my closest friends. Midway through the class I came to believe that I could no longer associate with the Christian church because of its oppressiveness, which was in sharp contrast to Jesus' liberating teachings.

This decision to become post-Christian required reevaluation of all my theological beliefs, including my beliefs about the Bible. At the beginning of my final semester of college I decided that much of the Bible, especially the writings of Paul, was too oppressive to be of use. I struggled for a long time with Paul's problematic teachings on issues such as women's leadership in the church and homosexuality. I went through a phase in which I tried to explain away their problematic nature via arguments such as "Back in Paul's time it was customary for women to be silent in public, so that passage isn't really relevant for today," or "The concept of a wholesome, committed same-sex relationship didn't exist in the first century, so Paul isn't speaking about homosexuality as it exists now," but eventually these arguments seemed to stretch the text in ways it did not want to stretch—these arguments were being untrue to the text and violated the text in ways I no longer wished to accept.

So instead of clinging to these arguments I rejected them, and thus rejected the text as well after acknowledging that without these faulty interpretations it was, indeed, oppressive. The Bible, as a whole, was no longer a sacred text in my life.

At the same time I was taking the Religion Senior Seminar, which focused on narrative theology. I was quickly drawn to narrative theology's view of the faith community as one that perpetuates itself via its stories. This theological framework made sense to me as I thought about how influential books had been throughout my life, and it gave me language to explain the powerful experiences I had had with Mennonite literature—Mennonite literature came out of the faith community, and Godde was present in the faith community, thus Godde was also present in the writing that members (however marginal) of the faith community produced. Because these texts had Godde in them, and more importantly because I experienced Godde through them, they were sacred to me. I also realized that Godde could be present in texts that originate in communities other than my own. This realization was crucial for me because it made me aware of the possibility of encountering Godde in anything I read.

Naming My Sacred Texts

In the time that has passed since then I have begun actively naming my sacred texts and doing my best to stay in touch with them via semi-frequent readings. I am continually amazed at how much I continue to learn from texts that I have read five or six times before. My current list of sacred texts includes (but is certainly not limited to), in no particular order, Chaim Potok's *My Name Is Asher Lev*,[14] *Rhubarb* magazine, *Mennonite Quarterly Review*,[15] the motion picture "High Fidelity,"[16] Jeff Gundy's "The Cookie Poem,"[17] and Rudy Wiebe's *The Blue Mountains of China*.

I will now briefly discuss the latter two texts to illustrate what makes a text "sacred" to me. Here is "The Cookie Poem" in its entirety:

"Here are my sad cookies."
The sad cookies. The once and future cookies.
The broken sweet cookies. The cookies
of heartbreaking beauty. The stony cookies
of Palestine. The gummy and delicious
olive and honey cookie. The pasty
damp cookie trapped in the child's hand.
Sad cookies, weird cookies, slippery
and dangerous cookies. Brilliant helpless

soiled and torn cookies, feverish and sweaty
cookies. Sullen cookies, sassy cookies,
the cookies of tantrum and the cookie of joy
and the sweet dark cookie of peace.
The faithful cookie of Rotterdam. The wild-eyed
cookie of Muenster. The salty Atlantic cookie.
Cookies in black coats, in coveralls,
in business suits, cookies in bonnets
and coverings and heels, cookies scratching
their heads and their bellies, cookies utterly
and shamelessly naked before the beloved.
Cookies of the Amish division, cookies
of the Wahlerhof, cookies of Zurich and
Strasburg and Volhynia and Chortitza,
Nairobi Djakarta Winnipeg Goshen.
Cookies who hand their children off
to strangers, who admonish their sons
to remember the Lord's Prayer, cookies
who say all right, baptize my children
and then sneak back to the hidden church anyway.
Cookies who cave in utterly. Cookies
who die with their boots on. Cookies
with fists, and with contusions.
The black-hearted cookie. The cookie with issues.
Hard cookies, hot cookies, compassionate
conservative cookies, cookies we loathe
and love, cookies lost, fallen, stolen,
crushed, abandoned, shunned. Weary
and heroic cookies, scathingly noted cookies,
flawed cookies who did their best.
Single cookies, queer cookies, cookies of color,
homeless cookie families sleeping in the car,
obsolete cookies broken down on the information
highway. Sad cookies, silent cookies,
loud cookies, loved cookies, your cookies
my cookies our cookies, all cookies
God's cookies, strange sweet hapless cookies
marked each one by the Imago Dei,
oh the Father the Son the Mother the Daughter
and the Holy Ghost all love cookies,
love all cookies, God's mouth is full
of cookies, God chews and swallows and flings

hands wide in joy, the crumbs fly
everywhere, oh God loves us all.

"The Cookie Poem" is an incredibly rich text. It gives a wonderful
retelling of Anabaptist-Mennonite history, acknowledging both the heroes ("The faithful cookie of Rotterdam") and villains ("The wild-eyed /
cookie of Muenster") of the faith community. It does not neatly define
the faith community but recognizes all of the spread-out voices and experiences that Mennonitism has to offer. Gundy recognizes humanity's
imperfections both in the past ("Cookies of the Amish division") and
now in the twenty-first century ("obsolete cookies broken down on the
information / highway."), but is affirming of humanity nonetheless. His
depiction of "God" as a loving, accepting Cookie Monster is an excellent
summation of the poem's thrust—humanity messes up sometimes, and
other times gets things right, but either way Godde loves humanity and
has surrounded humanity with beauty, and that is what matters.[18]

"The Cookie Poem" is sacred to me because it is a profound reminder of how life is made beautiful by Godde's love. The poem ener-
gizes me whenever I read it and keeps me mindful of the need to play my
part in the faith community so that there will be fewer "black-hearted
cookies" and more "sweet dark cookies of peace."

Wiebe's *The Blue Mountains of China* is much less hopeful than "The
Cookie Poem" but still touches me in a powerful way. It traces the story of
an extended Russian Mennonite family from the 1880s through Canada's
centennial year, 1967. Some of the family's members go to Canada and
prosper, some remain in Russia and are sent to Siberia, and some end up
in Paraguay. The central question of the book, which all of the characters
grapple with to one extent or another, is "What actions must one take if
one is a true follower of Jesus?" The answer Wiebe gives is that one must
sacrifice oneself for the good of others.[19] As the book's Christ figure, John
Reimer, says, one must "Hate your life. Just a little, more."[20]

I must admit that there is still a part of me that is drawn to this traditional Mennonite lust for martyrdom. Although in the end I reject
Wiebe's ethic of self-sacrifice, I find that each time I read *The Blue
Mountains of China* I have to wrestle with it anew; it intrigues me too
much to dismiss it outright. Even though I disagree with many of the
characters' decisions, reading about them always moves me deeply and
makes me want to remain in dialogue with the faith community.

As both *The Blue Mountains of China* and "The Cookie Poem" do, many of my sacred texts keep me connected in some way to the faith community. They provide an unofficial voice for the faith community, and I find that it is easier for me to dialogue with this voice than with voices from within the institutional church. Many of my sacred texts also reveal Godde's presence in the world to me and remind me that it is healthy to struggle with what that presence means for my life. I believe that sacred texts should help foster a liberating relationship with Godde. The Bible no longer does this for me, but my sacred texts do.

Notes

1. I use "sacred texts" rather than "scripture" because I find that for many people scripture denotes only the Bible or other "holy" texts such as the Quran or Talmud. Since my "scripture" does *not* include much of the Bible but instead includes various non-religious texts, I find it necessary to use a broader term, hence sacred texts.

2. Borrowing from some contemporary feminist writers, I use "Godde" rather than "God" because Godde points to the multi-gendered nature of the deity which it names, whereas God implies maleness because of the existence of its female counterpart goddess.

3. Collier, "Black-eyed Susan, Poet Laureate, 'Maryland, My Maryland!'" *American Poet* (Spring 2003): 9-13.

4. Wiebe, *The Blue Mountains of China* (Toronto: McClelland & Stewart, 1970); Gundy, "The Cookie Poem" in *Rhapsody With Dark Matter* (Huron: Bottom Dog Press, 2000): 52-53.

5. Today Lancaster Mennonite High School is part of the larger, multi-campus Lancaster Mennonite School (LMS) system, which offers grades kindergarten-12. LMS uses the Lancaster Mennonite High School (LMHS) name to refer only to grades 9-12, offered at the Lancaster Campus.

6. One mistranslation Mr. Sauder pointed out to us was of the Hebrew word *ratsach* in Exodus 20:13, which is the sixth commandment, traditionally translated as "thou shalt not kill." Mr. Sauder noted that the literal meaning of *ratsach* is "to dash against a stone violently," thus a better translation would be "thou shalt not murder."

7. Lewis, *Mere Christianity* (New York: Macmillan, 1960); Chambers *My Utmost for His Highest* (New York: Dodd, Mead & Company, 1935); Merton, *New Seeds of Contemplation* (Norfolk, Conn.: New Connections, 1962). These three texts were especially influential during this time.

8. John Howard Yoder, 1st. ed. (Grand Rapids: Eerdmans, 1972).

9. Trible, *Texts of Terror: Literary-Feminist Readings of Biblical Narratives*, Overtures to Biblical Theology 13 (Philadelphia: Fortress Press, 1984).

10. I have written about my experience of this lecture in "How Julia Kasdorf Changed My Life," *Goshen College Bulletin* 86:2 (June 2001): 10-11. This essay was written for Ervin Beck's Mennonite Literature course, described below. A revised text of the lecture itself can be found in Kasdorf's *The Body and the Book* (Baltimore: Johns Hopkins Press, 2001): 121-142.

11. For much of college I was planning on becoming a churchman, and Bender was my role model in envisioning how I wanted this vocation to unfold.

12. I was thrilled second semester of my junior year when I encountered J. Denny Weaver's *Anabaptist Theology in the Face of Postmodernity* (Telford, Pa.: Pandora Press U.S., 2000), which makes an attempt to put forth an Anabaptist theology influenced by concepts from various liberation theologies.

13. The specific texts that I am referring to are the following: Bergen, *Sitting Opposite My Brother* (Winnipeg: Turnstone Press, 1993); Wiebe, *The Blue Mountains of China*; Gundy, *Rhapsody With Dark Matter* (Huron: Bottom Dog Press, 2000); Brandt, *questions i asked my mother* (Winnipeg: Turnstone Press, 1987); Waltner-Toews (with Jean Janzen and Yorifumi Yaguchi), *Three Mennonite Poets* (Intercourse, Pa.: Good Books, 1986); Kasdorf, *Sleeping Preacher* (Pittsburgh: University of Pittsburgh Press, 1992), and *Eve's Striptease* (Pittsburgh: University of Pittsburgh Press, 1998). Gundy's essay appears in *Migrant Muses: Mennonite/s Writing in the U.S.,* ed. Ervin Beck and John D. Roth (Goshen, Ind.: Mennonite Historical Society, 1998): 23-30.

14. New York: Fawcett Columbine, 1972.

15. *Rhubarb* is a magazine of Mennonite writing published by the Mennonite Literary Society. *Mennonite Quarterly Review* is the journal of the Mennonite Historical Society.

16. "High Fidelity," directed by Stephen Frears, book by Nick Hornby, screenplay by D.V. DeVincentis, Steve Pink, John Cusack, and Scott Rosenberg (Touchstone Pictures, 2000).

16. From *Rhapsody With Dark Matter* (Huron: Bottom Dog Press, 2000): 53. Used by permission, all rights reserved.

17. One either loves "The Cookie Poem" or hates it. One example of this hatred is found in a review of *Rhapsody With Dark Matter* by Maurice Mierau, who writes, "I worry too about Gundy getting cute, for example in 'The Cookie Poem' … God as cookie monster? This seems arch and cloying at the same time." "Matter Dark With Rhapsody." *Rhubarb* 8 (Winter 2002): 40-41.

19. Ervin Beck notes that this answer was strongly influenced by Wiebe's relationship with John Howard Yoder in "The Politics of Rudy Wiebe in *The Blue Mountains of China.*" *Mennonite Quarterly Review* 73:4 (October 1999): 723-749.

20. Wiebe, *The Blue Mountains of China*, 259.

CHAPTER 14

Theological Breakdown, Rebuilding, and Hope

Benjamin Beachy

One recent Sunday morning my wife Sarah and I taught the three-and four-year-old Sunday school class at our congregation in Harrisonburg, Virginia. The Bible story for the day came from Acts 9—Paul's encounter with Jesus on the Damascus road—but of course the kids did not know that. They were just having fun talking about bright lights, then proving the point by shining flashlights in each others' eyes.

I am not sure Craig or Tim or Sonya could even define the term *Scripture*, let alone talk meaningfully about scriptural interpretation. Yet as they played with the flashlights and the wooden story figures they were interacting with the Bible—and they were interpreting Scripture through their interaction with it. If my memories are any guide, these early interactions with Scripture will shape their understanding of the Bible for years to come.

Certainly some of my earliest interactions with Scripture occurred in a Sunday school classroom. I remember sitting in a room, much as the children did the morning we talked about Paul's Damascus road experience, listening to an adult talk about Peter, David, Moses, and the rest. It is hard to say how much I absorbed from those classes, but I suspect that my mental image of Jesus still has bits of fuzz hanging off of it from Sunday school flannelgraphs.

Childlike Faith

As a child I developed an understanding of Scripture that could best be described as, well, childlike. This is not to say that it was simplistic, though many understand the term in that way. When Paul wrote that as a child he thought and acted as a child, he did not mean that childlike faith was less valuable than more mature, more adult beliefs. Jesus pointed out that childlike faith is often a blessing, at least where entry to the kingdom of God is concerned.

My childlike faith was founded on the then-unconscious assumption that I knew little about the world. Every day my parents did things that mystified me: They talked of things and people and events that were completely beyond my comprehension. It was perfectly natural to assume that if President Reagan could engage in supply-side economics, Jesus could walk on water—both were totally outside my comprehensible, childhood world. Undoubtedly, my comfort with things I could not understand was due in large part to my relationship with my parents. Had they been distant or capricious I likely would have had more trouble accepting the unknowable in such a laissez-faire way. Their love and acceptance inclined me to embrace their faith without question.

As a child I made no distinction between my interpretation of Scripture and my faith—the two were one and the same. The Bible was the Word of God, and it told us everything we needed to know about—as British comic writer Douglas Adams would say—life, the universe, and everything. The idea of critically analyzing scriptural interpretive techniques, even the idea that there were such interpretive techniques, never crossed my mind.

Needless to say, such faith could not last forever. As I grew older and gained knowledge, if not wisdom, my faith—and by extension my understanding of Scripture—encountered questions it was not prepared to answer. It was not sufficient to answer objections about the permanence of death by pointing out that Jesus raised Lazarus and that proved the point. Answers could not always begin with "The Bible says. . . . "

Seeking Logical Buttresses

My response to an increasing number of faith-based objections to things in the world that seemed self-evident was to seek out logical buttresses to faith. I wanted to prove that my faith had merit, to demonstrate logically, precisely, and definitively that everything I was taught as a child was more than just a figment of the imagination. I believed the Bible to be God's own Truth, and I wanted a tool to convince others. That better minds than mine had tried and failed to find the ultimate proof of faith was insignificant; I would succeed where they had failed— God willing.

I found the study of modern, intellectual apologetics fascinating, almost seductively so. I pored over C. S. Lewis and Francis Schaeffer. I dissected Augustine and reviewed the writings of early Anabaptists. I studied hard, thought hard, even prayed hard, but the truth I was looking for remained elusive. Eventually, I stumbled on the idea that there was more than one way of interpreting the Bible. It was, I realized, conceivable— though obviously wrong—that what the Bible said was not always what the Bible meant. Moreover, it was possible that perfectly sincere, faithful Christians could honestly disagree over the meaning of Scripture. The very idea of such deep disagreement frightened me.

In retrospect, all that fear seems a bit silly. The signs were there from the beginning. In the 1980s, when I was growing up, the Mennonite church was wrestling with the legacy of the 1960s and 1970s. Church membership became a hot-button issue as divorced individuals and those active in military service expressed their desire to be part of the church. Women were asking increasingly pointed questions about their role in the church, and the authority of bishops was being challenged. Everyone, it seemed, was arguing about the meaning of Scripture. It was a tumultuous time, and a great many people were disagreeing about a great many things. My ordered, tidy understanding of Scripture was bound to shatter.

As a child I saw chaos and confusion in plurality; when faced with a choice between the diversity and pluralism of contemporary Christianity and the comfort of a static, self-sufficient understanding of Scripture, I chose the latter. I was afraid of the uncertainty of diversity and of the dissolution of my well-organized faith. I began to read the Bible with a new fervor, drawing on the early Anabaptists for inspiration. I felt myself a direct spiritual descendant of those early rebaptizers. I sought to make their zeal and passion and assured conviction my own.

As I interacted with Scripture, however, I brought with me cultural and philosophical influences about which the early Anabaptists never dreamed. I lived in a world where the Enlightenment had borne its fruit in full, where the optimism of the modern age had given way to nihilism and despair, where the enemy of faith was not heresy but agnosticism. I could not simply adopt the interpretive approach of the Anabaptists wholesale—it did not match my culture. Instead, I found I needed to revise and adapt the Anabaptists' teachings to meet my own needs and questions.

Adaptation in Stages

I began the process of adaptation as a conservative. I wanted to preserve what was good and valuable within the Anabaptist tradition and modify only that which did not apply to contemporary life. I quickly realized, however, that this approach allowed too much room for change—it conceded too much to pluralism. As this conviction deepened I began to move from mere conservativism toward fundamentalism.

My reading habits changed. I took an interest in creation science—the belief in the science of biblical creation accounts as literally true—and read anything on the subject I could find. I continued to read the Bible voraciously, but I appropriated the interpretive approach of creation science for other purposes. I adopted the deliberately simplistic, literal view of Scripture popular among creation scientists, an approach that led me to conclude that since Jesus rose from the dead in three days, the universe must have been created in six. I believed—or rather, I willed myself to believe—that this interpretive approach was not only the right one, it was the only one. I told myself that every other way of interpreting Scripture was manipulative; every other interpreter was corrupt and sought to distort God's Word for his or her own selfish ends.

The proper interpretive approach, I told myself, was to bring the mind, the soul, and the biblical text together and allow the Spirit to move. One needed merely to be open to the presence of God and the true and simple meaning of the text would make itself evident. Overanalyzing Scripture or exposing it to scholarly criticism corrupted the interpretive process. Simplicity was the best way because God would surely give us his word in a clear and unambiguous format.

I was, of course, aware of problematic texts, and I generally dealt with them by trivializing their importance. The fact that many women in the church declined to wear a head covering, for example, despite

Paul's clear dictates on the matter, was insignificant—at worst, perhaps, a concession to human sinfulness. Problem areas that were too large to ignore, such as the first few chapters of Genesis, I resolved by adapting cultural "truths" to match the biblical text. Obviously, I reasoned, paleontologists had the record wrong because the Bible clearly states that a catastrophic global flood occurred.

I was vaguely aware of the arrogance of this approach—I was effectively claiming that my opinion was the really important one—but I reasoned that God demanded holiness of us, and the light must not commune with darkness. What I was not aware of was the depth of my own hypocrisy.

A Theological Breakdown

During my time in college a series of events systematically demolished my carefully constructed interpretational frameworks. I was forced to confront the deceit and the fear that buttressed my beliefs. I was forced to critically examine the ways I interpreted Scripture. I was forced—and this was the hardest of all—to admit that I was wrong about many things.

My theological breakdown began in my home congregation. It was a fairly small church where my father was serving in his second full-time pastorate. Over time it became apparent that the congregation was deeply divided over the nature and role of congregational leadership. Congregational meetings and even Sunday services became protracted power struggles as factions within the congregation vied for dominance. Under normal circumstances conference leaders could have stepped in and lent their impartial authority to the mediation process. Conference officials, however, were themselves struggling with a caustic debate on homosexuality within the church and had little time or energy to devote to congregational crises. Left largely alone, the congregation eventually splintered.

My father's experience and, to varying degrees, those of the rest of my family, showed me the heart of a congregation gone horribly wrong. Church had always been a safe place for me; in some cases the church building was literally a second home. Watching others betray my father—as I then understood the situation—shattered my confidence in what I had believed to be a place of safety.

My world continued to turn in unpredictable ways as changes that began at home intensified during my Eastern Mennonite University-required cross-cultural experience. I entered Mennonite Voluntary Service, and, for a year, I lived and worked among people who daily demonstrated the gospel in action—people whose hermeneutic was physical and practical, not academic. They practiced what I believed, yet their understanding of the Bible was often at odds with mine.

At the same time I was corresponding with a close friend who was even more fundamentalist than I. She had scriptural interpretation down pat, but her model of Christian service was handing out tracts in an airport. She lived in a suburban world shielded from poverty and spiritual need. From her privileged position she criticized those on the front lines of service because their theology was not orthodox enough.

In the end the tension proved to be too much. I had pinned much of my scriptural interpretive approach on fundamentalism, but fundamentalism held little relevance for the poor and oppressed. I had always depended on the church to provide shelter and security, but the church had offered me dissension and division. Those I trusted to support me had abandoned me.

Rebuilding, with God's Help

It has taken years to rebuild theologically from my breakdown. I am still far from finished, but I have found God's faithfulness along the way.

Today my faith is founded on relationships: relationships with God, Scripture, my local congregation, and God's kingdom in this world.

Today I am open to the possibility that I may disagree with any of those I relate to. I am exploring disagreement as a healthy part of growth.

Today I am committed to own Scripture as a looking glass. I want to relate to Scripture in a way that over time reveals my true character and the true character of God.

Today I am looking for new ways of relating to Scripture, new interpretive techniques that reveal more of the text's complexities.

Today I am watching for Christ in those around me. I am seeking Christ in the biblical text, and beyond the biblical text.

Today I am being sustained by the community of faith.

Today I am anticipating tomorrow, because I want to meet God there.

CHAPTER 15

Weaving Yarns and Telling Sacred Stories

Malinda Elizabeth Berry

When I first began thinking carefully about my own journey with Scripture, I discovered I had a great deal of energy for asking loads of questions about various notions of authority when it comes to the Bible.[1] The more I tried to figure out where all that energy was coming from, the more I realized that in the Mennonite communities where I have grown up, worshiped, and preached, we tend to grant the Bible privilege and power over us almost too quickly. We assume that somehow our lives as "God's people" in the twenty-first century are linked to the lives of "God's people" who now exist only on pages of paper bound together with glue and called a holy book. As "People of the Book," we ought to wonder, Who forged that link? Who wrote those words? Who dreamed up the idea of putting them all together into one hefty volume?

The best way I know how to answer these questions is to tell stories. Those stories may not always be on point, but when we think of them as colorful strands of yarn or thread that are warp and woof, this imagery resonates with the psalmist who declares, "For it was you who formed my inward parts; you knit me together in my mother's womb. . . . My frame was not hidden from you, when I was being made in secret, intricately woven in the depths of the earth" (Ps. 139:13, 15).

I am training to become a systematic theologian. One of the things this means to me is that I have permission to ask lots of tough questions because I have a responsibility to interrogate both my own and my faith community's faith claims. Right now, I want to know more and ask questions about what we believe about the "authority of Scripture."

Underlying my reflections in this telling of my story about Scripture is a desire to be self-aware and self-conscious about both my agenda and my desire to be faithful to biblical Christian faith. I appreciate this helpful reminder from biblical scholar Walter Brueggemann:

> How each of us reads the Bible is partly the result of family, neighbors, and friends (a socialization process), and partly the God-given accident of long-term development in faith. Consequently the real issues of biblical authority and interpretation are not likely to be settled by cognitive formulations or by appeals to classic confessions. These issues live in often unrecognized, uncriticized, and deeply powerful ways—especially if they are rooted (as they may be for most of us) in hurt, anger, or anxiety.[2]

Wrestling with Authority

Like the biblical text, our lives and our relationships are not filled with days of poetic bliss. God's words of love and justice that *speak us* and *speak to us* require struggle in the tradition of Jacob's struggle with God's messenger at Peniel in Genesis 32. And so, many Christians wrestle with what it means to call the Bible "God's word." Struggling for real meaning while honoring the integrity of Scripture and listening with open hearts to the message being spoken through this book is a difficult task and should be understood as a journey, not a destination. Committing to this struggle for finding meaning in Christian Scripture also means committing to the "authority of Scripture."

In an article based on interviews she had with women about the role of authority and the authority of Scripture in their lives, Brazilian feminist theologian Ivone Gebara writes, "For them, linking the Bible and authority seemed rather strange. For many of them, authority is something that belongs to an outside power exercised over their lives, to a coercive force. . . . The Bible seemed apart from such experiences."[3] One of the women Gebara spoke with responded to her questions by simply saying, "If I don't know something, that thing can't have any real authority in my life.'"[4] In the life of the church and in the lives of its members, an increasing number of things are clamoring to be authoritative, and if we do not know the Bible, then how can it mean anything to us?

Returning to a sense of the sacred that is contrasted with the profane is one way I think we can begin to invite people to travel toward the Bible. I am not referring here to some kind of empty spirituality or self-congratulatory piety. I am talking about recovering, even taking back from the wider culture, a sense of holiness and reverence for people, ideas, and texts—both written and spoken—in ways that keep them from becoming bought and sold.

One application of this comes from Elisabeth Schüssler Fiorenza, who argues that a feminist hermeneutic striving to be multi-vocal must cross the boundaries of the biblical canon as it identifies its sacred texts. This points to a second layer of definition of what Scripture is: a collection of sacred texts that are not exclusively biblical texts. They are sacred because they help a community of people make meaning of their lives and interactions, giving them images to use as they imagine the nature of their collective and individual destinies.

Setting Doctrinal Terms

In the tradition of the Wesleyan Quadrilateral, I think of Scripture as one of four sources that we draw upon when we formulate our theology and ethics; the other sources are reason, tradition, and experience. In this sense, Scripture has authority because we look to it with the expectation that it contains a message that provides guidance and will illuminate discussion around tough questions of discipleship. But to what end? The Bible's function is to give people who acknowledge and worship God a written account of the stories of God's people in times that—while distant and remote—resonate with some of our contemporary experiences as we study, interpret, and reflect on who and how God is for us today.

That is why "Scripture" is more than a book. Somehow, it points to a transcendent and yet incarnational God, and as this is experienced, a story unfolds. That story necessarily overlaps with the Bible's characters and events, but what is different is that these areas of overlap are embodied by real people who experience God's vindication, Jesus' challenges, Wisdom's clarity, or "Holy Presence" in *this* time and in contexts which make sense to us. Thus we who bear the inscription of God's goodness, honor God's holiness, are obedient to God's law, and welcome God as stranger bring the Bible to life and create Scripture.

This, then, is part of what makes these texts (the pages of the Bible and our very lives) sacred. In this process, we collapse reason, tradition, and experience into a way of being that only makes sense when measured according to standards established by communities who read and interpret the biblical texts. Implicit in this last statement is my conviction that the Bible is a reliable source for the narratives of God's people in days long gone. Their sacredness comes not from the exact words of the text but from the one to whom these stories point: God our Creator, Redeemer, and Sustainer.

By giving Scripture an organic definition, its authority is no longer something to fear. Like the woman Gebara interviewed, we as church communities cannot—indeed, ought not—give authority to Scripture unless it is something we know. Moreover, we cannot be abused (as easily) by something that is a part of us. Returning to Gebara's observations, if we as believers are part of Scripture, then Scripture has authority. The locus of that authority is found inside both the community (collective) and its members (individuals).

But how can one locus exist in two places? I think this points to the tenuous nature of authority. If we are unable to live with "shared" authority, which I believe any authority granted by humans must be, then there is a good chance we have shifted from Scripture's intent and authoritative function: to draw people in toward God and toward one another through testimony which reveals struggle, liberation, and reconciliation according to the witness of God's mission in the world given not only by Jesus Christ but the cloud of witnesses who have been part of Scripture.

Making Connections and Commitments

I must admit that I think of myself as a recovering biblical illiterate. Growing up in a heavily populated Mennonite area of the United States in the light and shadows of well-known church institutions may make my disclosure seem a bit shocking. Even worse, though, is the fact that I was very attentive in my Mennonite Sunday school classes and quite a good student at the Mennonite high school and college I attended. As I think back on those experiences, I must also confess that I got away with being biblically illiterate not because the Bible was ignored, but because I thought I was beyond the Bible and memorizing Scripture was not my idea of time well spent.

By the time I was in my early teen years, I did not want to hear any more Bible stories because my valiant Sunday school teachers—armed with denominational Sunday school materials—just kept telling the same old stories over and over. I knew all those stories already, my reasoning went, so I stopped paying attention to the Bible. During my second year of high school, our Sunday school teacher tried his best to get us excited about studying the Old Testament; this was the summer after our previous teacher tried to get us to read the book of Revelation. We needed to understand Israel's history, our teacher declared. Cynical youth that I was, I blew off this admonition with a, "Well, I'm not Jewish, and besides, all we Mennonites care about is the New Testament." With that, I turned my back on the Bible again.

I remember one occasion, also during high school, when for a reason I no longer remember, I was trying to find the "Christmas Story" in the synoptic gospels. I did not find a neat and tidy version of "The Nativity" as I had expected. That made me mad. I felt I had been lied to because I had thought the version of "Christmas" I had heard every December was in the Bible in one complete narrative.

As I reflect on this episode, I think that based on my adolescent logic I felt as though I had been betrayed because what I thought was real was actually someone's imagining. That could and should have been a good thing. Instead I wanted to know why St. Francis could imagine the crèche but I was not allowed to imagine Paul as a crusty old man I did not need to listen to or God as a female-ish entity or Jesus as a jolly, short, chubby Palestinian guy instead of that emaciated weakling dressed in white on my Grandma and Grandpa Hostetler's wall. Why was someone else's imagining of what the text means more credible than mine? As time went by, this struggle continued but with clearer political overtones. After the light-bulb flash of learning that the psalmist describing the Good Shepherd was not talking about Jesus, I realized I could ask more demanding questions of the tradition surrounding portrayals of women in the Bible. Why, for example, did everyone think Mary Magdalene was a prostitute or that she was in love with Jesus?

By the time I had graduated from high school, I was sure of one thing about the Bible: I had had it with patriarchy, which seemed to be most insidious in the church and its interpretation of the "Word of God." I was appalled that Lot was going to "feed" his daughters to the ruffians pounding at his door, troubled that David was still a "great king" even though he had crafted a major plot against Bathsheba and Uriah, and horrified by the sad story of Tamar's rape. There were a few things about the Bible my Sunday school teachers forgot to tell me—especially about what I perceived as the Bible's shadow side.

Despite my resistance to the biblical text due to its bad parts, I found myself trying to commit to reading the Bible. These off-on commitments took the form of New Year's resolutions. I figured that as the owner of four Bibles I ought to at least read one version of the text from cover to cover. Moreover, in all my raging against the patriarchal biblical machine, I had to admit that I really did not know the Bible. I struggled to make sense of what I was reading not only theologically but literally as well. All of those hard-to-pronounce names and places, slain lambs, floods. What was it all about? After about a month or so, I would inevitably give up my resolve to know the Bible better. Looking back, I think I feared that if I really read and studied this set of texts, I might decode the gospel message as dramatically as Paul, and I was not ready for that much transformation.

In college, I loved my religion and ethics courses. Delving into issues and ethics that allowed me to pontificate and posture was an important stage of development for me. However, I neglected to develop a reverence for the sacred nature of the texts I studied. The Bible functioned as tool—nothing less, nothing more. I was able to move beyond this stage of my journey when I decided to go to Associated Mennonite Biblical Seminary.

Attending seminary was a watershed experience for me. I found a place where I could ask tough questions of the biblical text and also—through worship and study—experience the Bible as the sacred *Words* of God. I would go down into the book stacks in the library and pore over volumes that helped me voice my questions. The power and sacredness of the Bible emerged from my decision to finally pay closer attention to this book after all these years.

When I chose to begin paying attention, I learned about the story of Queen Vashti. We find Vashti's story in the book of Esther 1:9-22. In fourteen verses, this woman makes quite an impression on readers. She is married to Ahasuerus, king of the Persian empire, and one evening he sends some eunuchs to bring Vashti into his presence. The queen refuses to go because she knows Ahasuerus has been eating and drinking to the point of overindulgence. His summons is merely a way for him to show her off in front of his male guests, and the narrative tells us that she will not be handled in such a vulgar manner. Because of her choice to disobey Ahasuerus, she is no longer a queen. In her reflections on this part of Esther, Sidnie White Crawford writes,

> The character of Vashti the Queen serves as a foil to Esther the Queen, and very different fates await each. . . . The minute she opposes her husband the king, the entire machinery of the state descends on [Vashti's] head and she loses all status and power. To many modern commentators, Vashti is a feminist hero, opposing the male power structure with what little independence she has. . . . However, in the story, Vashti fails, and Esther succeeds. What message is the author trying to convey? Can we reconcile that message to our differing ideas about the status and role of women in society?[5]

In my own life, Vashti has become an increasingly important figure for three reasons. First, she *is* a feminist hero for me. She urges me to remain steadfast in my commitments to working for "gender justice." Second, Vashti reminds me that this work is not without sacrifice. Through the example of this Persian queen, I must ask, "Am I ready to pay the price for being faithful to God's *shalom* when it comes to integrity and building right relationships?" Finally, Vashti is a woman of action. Esther is bold in her willingness to risk so much for others, but unlike her predecessor, her methods are not those of the activist. As a woman of color, I am challenged by Vashti's story not only to know and remember my own worth but to have the courage to tell others who I am.

I come from a privileged class and a privileged family, so I have never looked to the Bible as a source of liberation from the struggle of material poverty. But I also have stories from my family that have stirred in me a deep commitment to women's liberation from sexism and patriarchy, including their socioeconomic dimensions. My commitment to this vision and the work it involves comes from experiences of anger and pain. As I study the stories of biblical women like Vashti and Bathsheba, I have come to look to the Bible as a place where I can find, and thus more fully trust, a God of women's work. My work is to study the Bible, my sacred text, full of stories about women who have survived and suffered and who have extended hospitality and hope.

In this place of questions and struggle, I have learned to see the Bible in narrative terms. I feel my greatest connection to the Bible when I approach it as an anthology, an edited collection of all kinds of writing by all sorts of authors. Yet I have no doubt that I have a "biblical faith." Thanks to my goodly heritage, I am not about to give up on the Bible; rather, I must confess my strong desire to convert others to my way of reading and living with this book. I want us all to be allowed to imagine and read out in the open and not be accused of heresy, apostasy, being New Age, or just generally being un-Christian. I find myself reacting against the rigidity of Christians who equate knowing the Bible with having faith, as if slapping a Bible verse on a conviction makes it Christian, whereas failure to back one's view in this way is evidence of secularism.

On the other hand, I have concerns about the outright rejection of the Bible and biblical religion, a reality in some circles. I find Schüssler Fiorenza's articulation of this dynamic helpful. She writes,

A postbiblical feminist stance is in danger of becoming ahistorical and apolitical. It too quickly concedes that women have no authentic history within biblical religion and too easily relinquishes women's feminist biblical heritage. Nor can such a stance do justice to the positive experiences of contemporary women within biblical religion. It must either neglect the influence of biblical religion on women today or declare women's adherence to biblical religion as "false consciousness." . . . Feminists cannot afford such an ahistorical or antihistorical stance because it is precisely the power of oppression that deprives people of their history.[6]

Now as I read the Bible, feminist and womanist[7] perspectives often function as my primary interpretive lenses. The gift of these perspectives to me is courage. As I study, more important to me than satisfying my christological questions has been the cultivation of women role models from the stories of Scripture—women like Vashti, the Cannanite woman, and Martha who know their worth. When it comes to the Bible, then, these women become us and we become them.

We are Vashti. With our heads held high, we will not be party to men's manipulations. We are Bathsheba. We are angry because the powerful stole from us what they had no right to even touch. We are the Cannanite woman. We seek justice for those close to us, knowing that even men are not above reproach. We are Martha. We fuss over details *and* we are committed to Jesus' moral vision. We are these women. And we have survived. And we will continue to live on into the future because our stories and our lives are sacred.

Notes

1. Over the past decade I have thought extensively about my understanding of Scripture, but the first Journeys with Scripture colloquy, which took place at Laurelville Mennonite Church Center in June 2002 prompted my further thinking in these directions. This chapter is a slightly edited version of those reflections as recorded in *Telling Our Stories: Personal Engagements with Scripture,* ed. Ray Gingerich and Earl Zimmerman (Telford, Pa.: Cascadia Publishing House, 2006).

2. Walter Brueggemann, "Biblical Authority: A Personal Reflection," *Christian Century* (January 3-10, 2001): 15.

3. Ivone Gebara, "What Scriptures are Sacred Authority? Ambiguities of the Bible in the Lives of Latin American Women,"*Concilium,* ed. Kwok Pui-Lan and Elisabeth Schüssler Fiorenza (June 1998): 7.

4. Ibid.

5. Sidnie White Crawford, "Esther," *The New Interpreter's Bible,* vol. 3 (Nashville: Abingdon Press, 1999): 883.

6. Elisabeth Schüssler Fiorenza, *In Memory of Her: A Feminist Theological Reconstruction of Christian Origins* (New York: Crossroad, 1998): xlviii-xlix.

7. For a treatment of how womanism interacts with the biblical text, see Delores Williams, *Sisters in the Wilderness: The Challenge of Womanist God-Talk* (Maryknoll, N.Y.: Orbis Books, 1993).

CHAPTER 16

Seeking Balance: Trusting in the Christ Behind the Scriptures

Ryan Beiler

My earliest memory of engaging Scripture is of my older sister telling me that Bible stories were actually true—that David and Goliath, Noah, Jonah, and all of those fantastic stories really happened. I must have been a skeptical four- or five-year-old, because though I do not remember the exact words we exchanged, I have the distinct impression that she was insistent and I resistant. Then there is a long stretch where I do not have any specific memories of my interaction with the Bible. I found church and Sunday school rather boring, as I suspect do most kids when in elementary or junior high school.

The Practice of Reading the Text

It was not until age fourteen—because of a somewhat typical but also miraculous altar call in response to which I made my personal commitment to follow Christ—that I took the initiative to engage Scripture for myself. I want to make clear that although the nature of the event was one that now makes me wince (emotional manipulation with a dash of brimstone) I did have a real and life-changing experience of God's love and forgiveness—an example of the Spirit working despite the questionable methods of the messenger.

It was through this experience and my subsequent baptism that I committed to daily Scripture reading and prayer. I started with the New Testament, one chapter a day. Since then I have maintained this daily discipline in varying forms, at times reading a chapter from both the Old and New Testaments, at times even three chapters a day. Although I have maintained some form of this discipline almost without interruption for the last thirteen years, I have also always taken a "sabbath" from daily readings from Friday evening through Sunday evening. I am now on my third or fourth trip through the entire Bible.

For the past few years, I have done the Daily Office Lectionary from the *Book of Common Prayer,* which incorporates morning and evening psalms with readings from the Old Testament, New Testament, and the Gospels. I have enjoyed the variety and breadth of the lectionary because it has helped me get in touch with the rhythms of the church year and has been a welcome shift from plowing through the Bible chapter-by-chapter. It is also a more constant reminder of the diversity within Scripture—especially the psalms, with their alternating battle hymns, cries for justice, celebrations, and laments.

For more than a decade, I have also participated in weekly small-group Bible studies in one form or another—starting in high school, then during summers while working at Spruce Lake Retreat and Wilderness Camp, at college, and in my various church settings. I say more about these experiences below.

From Plain to Nuanced Readings

I certainly started with a very plain reading of the Bible, even quasi-literalist—earnestly struggling with Jesus' admonition to pluck out one's eye if it offends thee (Matt. 5:29, KJV), which my teenage eyes often did. But this plain reading also led me to reject whatever civil religion I had picked up in eight years of public schooling and embrace for myself for the first time Jesus' clear teachings on peacemaking and non-violence. Until then it had been my parents' and church's teaching but not my own belief.

The summer I "got saved" and started reading the Bible was also the summer between public junior high and my first year at Lancaster Mennonite High School (LMHS)[1] in Lancaster, Pennsylvania. My first memory of cultivating a more nuanced view of Scripture comes from my senior year at LMHS, when I had a Bible class with Wilmer Heisey. He introduced the class to the idea that just because something is in the Bible does not mean it is right; in other words, some of Scripture is *description*, not *prescription*. This was specifically introduced in the context of "the Fall" and "the Curse" of humankind in Genesis. I think somewhere along the line we also discussed the concept of progressive revelation—that Old Testament war history had to be seen through the lens of the New Testament teachings of Christ. So things I had been reading in the Bible were getting a little more complex but also making more sense.

I also remember that that was about the time the Jesus Seminar emerged with its color-coded gospels, and that Mr. Heisey helped me process my response.[2] My response was mainly defensive; I was filled with frustration over the public credibility given to a project full of speculative interpretations and circular arguments. But without trying to debunk the Jesus Seminar in this essay, it is simply important to recognize that this project stood as my first serious encounter with, and response to, a threat to my understanding of biblical authority.

For most of my Bible-reading life at that point, my inquiry was focused mainly on interpretation, especially on controversial topics such as pacifism, feminism, homosexuality, and other hotly debated subjects. My inquiries into finding a biblical response to these topics presupposed the authority of Scripture as I weighed various hermeneutical approaches I encountered. I also enjoyed finding some of the crazy Old Testament stories I had never read or heard before and noting these discoveries in my journal as I reflected on the many messages of Scripture.

After graduating from a Mennonite high school, I went to Ithaca College—a secular school in Ithaca, New York—and in religious studies classes came into contact with more radical thinkers: Marc Ellis, Elisabeth Schüssler Fiorenza, John Dominic Crossan, Walter Wink, and others who even more directly challenged my presuppositions of scriptural authority. Although these more radical thinkers posed important questions, I viewed their scholarly and philosophical assumptions as very different from mine. I was seeking to follow and imitate Christ. And though their intellectual challenges caused significant struggle, my default Christian community at the time, Campus Crusade for Christ, was particularly conservative and allowed me to retain most of my assumptions about the Bible.

For the first few years at Ithaca, I was part of a Campus Crusade men's Bible study, which provided much longed-for fellowship and community and was more meaningful for its prayer time. The style of the leaders was rather rigid and dogmatic, following an outline that did not allow for much discussion on issues of interest to me; the leaders seemed really more interested in turning us into little evangelism machines.

Even though I valued the relationships I was building, I had a desire for radical discipleship that went well beyond the narrow conservative fundamentalism I experienced at Crusade. My faith was becoming more politicized as I read articles in *Sojourners* magazine and books by Gandhi, Martin Luther King Jr., the Berrigan brothers, Oscar Romero, and Ron Sider among others. I became both dissatisfied with Crusade's right-wing slant and its modernist, rationalist, apologist approach to the Bible's historicity, accuracy, and authority.

Critiquing the Bible
While Affirming the Text's Authority

Around this time I attended a peace conference at Eastern Mennonite University (EMU, in Harrisonburg, Va.) at which a student from another Mennonite school expressed to me her unwillingness to even consider the Bible as a source of authority because of its history of abuse in the hands of oppressive powers. While recognizing the truth of that history, I was also saddened that she was not willing to balance that perception with the Bible's equally valid history as containing a message of liberation. To me, it was a mistake to throw out the baby with the bath water, thus ceding Scripture to its corrupters.

I partly interpret the difference between her reaction and mine by acknowledging that we were both rebelling against our prevailing institutions. She was rebelling against a church institution that seemed hostile to her sense of justice; I was rebelling against a secular university environment that was hostile to my faith; we rejected or valued the Bible accordingly.

On my return to Ithaca after a semester in Central America through EMU's cross-cultural program, I had had enough of Crusade and started a social justice Bible study with a friend at neighboring Cornell University. We approached justice issues through the lens of Scripture, exploring the many interpretations of its content while implicitly affirming its authority as our guide in matters of social concern and justice.

It is probably only since coming to *Sojourners* (where I edit *Sojo-Mail)* that I have seriously and directly examined questions of biblical authority itself: Where did the Bible actually come from? How was it inspired? Why should we believe it or follow it? Bringing these questions into two different dating relationships provided the context for deeper questioning on these issues. These questions were important to ask in those relationships both because of a mutual desire to see if our views were compatible and my own desire to articulate my deepest beliefs. The fact that biblical authority was an important question in both of these relationships also revealed to me how much of a core issue biblical authority was and is to my personal faith. These relationships also underscored for me both the value of community and honest dialogue in one's approach to the Bible.

I started my more intentional study of the nature of Scripture itself by reading Anabaptist authors. As I did, I found that I resonated with the differences I recognized between them and fundamentalist/evangelical approaches and even liberal ones. I also found authors from other traditions with a more dynamic view of Scripture who at the same time retained a form of meaningful authority and orthodoxy that I value. I even convinced my small-group Bible study to take up the topic—although it can be hard to have an honest and probing discussion on this issue with the many people unwilling to examine their presuppositions, preferring instead to compile evidence to confirm their points of view.

In this process of exploration, it has become increasingly difficult for me to articulate my view of Scripture, especially in relation to issues of authority and inspiration. I recognize how different genres of Scripture demand that we use different approaches as we read, interpret, and apply them to our lives. The question of the Bible's origin is part of that reality. I have also found a useful, though of course not direct, parallel between the humanity and divinity of Christ and the human and divine origins of Scripture: there is a paradox that cannot be fully explained, making this a matter of faith.

Choices, Stories, and Truth

But the questions I have learned to ask keep surfacing. As I try to answer them, I seem to have three choices: (1) I can forthrightly reject a particular author or story (e.g. Paul's admonitions of submission for slaves and wives) and implicitly deny the authority of the text; (2) I can find an alternative interpretation for a problematic text that harmonizes with my opinion and salves my biblical conscience; (3) I can affirm the authority of Scripture, retain my dissonant opinion, and live with the tension of the contradictions. Choice 1 leaves me less accountable, and choice 2 leaves me less than satisfied. I find that I pretty much live in a space made by choice 3, which leaves me feeling incoherent and generally hard-pressed to explain myself.

At the same time, living with choice 3 has allowed me to become more comfortable with the more postmodern predilection for valuing "stories" over "truths." Valuing stories allows me to appreciate Scripture as a whole rather than worrying about troublesome historical details, like "If Adam and Eve and Cain and Abel were the first family, who did Cain marry?"

This does not mean that I discard the idea of truth. Instead, I have a framework for valuing the biblical story's major themes—such as the liberation and deliverance of ancient Israel—at the same time as I witness the present-day story of oppression faced by my Palestinian sisters and brothers. I can still say that the story—and the truth—that matters is that God loves the poor and the oppressed. I recognize that some may disagree with my interpretation of these stories. A contemporary illustration of this approach is the fact that a few of the events of my narrative here are out of chronological order in the interest of thematic coherence, but I do not think that diminishes the truth of *my* story.

I have, thankfully, been able to find within my church a community of self-described "evangelical" believers who take the whole of Scripture seriously—and not just as a proof-text for personal or political agendas—but also allow for deep questions, ambiguities, and struggles with particular passages, concepts, and authors (Paul has taken a lot of heat, for example). Having common ground upon which to grapple—even in disagreement—helps ease the frustration and isolation of the sort I experienced during my college years and beyond.

My current weekly Bible study has often had two unofficial parts. The first, which the majority of people attend, is generally a pretty standard discussion of a particular text, perhaps with some questions and context provide by a facilitator, followed by corporate prayer.

The second part, at times referred to as the "heretics' hour," is when most have gone home. A few of us linger to hash over the questions we were earlier unable to articulate—or too chicken to ask in front of the whole group. Pretty much anything is fair game by then, and there is as much laughter as anything else. I could hunt down some Scripture reference to compare this scenario to Jesus and his disciples, but that would be using the Bible to justify my preferences and practices, which is generally poor theology.

I guess what I have sought—and have found among authors, mentors, and friends—is permission to be neither fundamentalist nor liberal, to find an orthodox and thoroughly Anabaptist theology of Scripture that recognizes the Bible as inspired and authoritative but also as having been transmitted through imperfect human authors and institutions.

I have not found completely satisfying answers for the controversies that hinge on one's view of Scripture—such as homosexuality and the historical Jesus, to name just two hot buttons. But as a Christian, my allegiance above all is to Christ—who alone is the Word of God. So as I move away from an inerrantist view of the Bible that seems incompatible with history, common sense, and the very diversity of Scripture itself, I place my trust in him—as I come to know him through the working of the Holy Spirit, through his body present in the church community now and in history, and, yes, through the Scriptures that Spirit-guided community selected to tell his story.

Notes

1. Today Lancaster Mennonite High School is part of the larger, multi-campus Lancaster Mennonite School (LMS) system, which offers grades kindergarten-12. LMS uses the Lancaster Mennonite High School (LMHS) name to refer only to grades 9-12, offered at the Lancaster Campus.

2. Robert W. Funk, Roy W. Hoover, and The Jesus Seminar, *The Five Gospels: the Search for the Authentic Words of Jesus* (New York: MacMillan Publishing Company, 1993). *The Five Gospels* is a collective report of gospel scholars who were working at the question, "What did Jesus really say?" For words ascribed to Jesus by the biblical text, the authors used red ink when they perceived that the words were "most probably spoken by him"; pink when they were more certain the words had suffered modification or less certain they could be traced back to

Jesus; gray when they ascertained the words reflected Jesus' ideas but did not originate with him; and black when the words were deemed inauthentic, placed on his lips by admirers or enemies (ix-x). The text also includes the Gospel of Thomas, a non-canonical gospel that includes 114 sayings and parables attributed to Jesus, many of which have parallels within the canonical gospels.

Part Two

Responses
to the Journey

CHAPTER 17

On Observing Pilgrims

Nancy Tatom Ammerman

It is my job to be a "systematic observer." That is what sociologists do. We catch people in the act of living their lives, then back off to look again from a distance, searching for the otherwise hidden paths in the maze. Then we tell the tales—both about what the living looks like up close and about the path that surrounds and shapes it. What we too seldom talk about is how we came to be watching in the first place and what it felt like to us along the way. So let me tell you a little bit about where I was sitting when I noticed this particular bunch of pilgrims wandering by.

I moved to Boston, Massachusetts, three years ago and to Hartford, Connecticut, eight years before that. Ever since moving north I have desperately missed having a regular opportunity to study the Bible with a group of others who care about what it has to say and are willing to dig around in search of its meaning. In all my adult years before that, there had always been fellow travelers through Scripture, people with whom I marveled at its beauty, argued with its idiocy, and wrestled with its demands on my life. We have been lucky in these New England cities to find churches where the Bible seriously informs the preaching, but finding one that has adult Sunday school or weeknight Bible studies is another matter entirely! I know, I know—I could have taken the initiative to start a group myself, but I have not. And I have let my own personal reading of Scripture slide as well, buried under the avalanche of career and family responsibilities. So I watched the young pilgrims here with a healthy tug of guilt and a large measure of nostalgia.

Nostalgia because I identified with so much of what I heard in their stories. I, too, grew up doing my "daily Bible readings" (we did not call it a lectionary, but it was) and memorizing weekly verses in Sunday school. I not only learned to name all sixty-six books of the Bible, but I also could find any given passage faster than most any "sword drill" competitor around. By the time I was in junior high and active in Girls Auxiliary (the Southern Baptist mission organization for girls), I was memorizing whole chapters, Proverbs 31 being among the more daunting. I always took my Bible to church and never laid it on the floor. My father's sermons were laced with impromptu references to dozens of verses that would buttress his points, so it was important to have a Bible handy at all times. Like so many of the writers of these essays, I consciously remember little of the content from those days, but the words and images are powerful still.

The tug of guilt I felt in reading these stories might better be described as a nagging worry. You see, I have a daughter who is of just this age, and while I have no doubt that she knows a great deal about the Bible and holds its values close to her heart, I also know that she simply did not spend her early childhood so thoroughly immersed in words and images that can now be called up to guide her. I wish now that we and our church communities had been even more diligent in providing those biblical basics. Her experience probably falls somewhere between the intense biblical surroundings I experienced and the anemic platitudes many liberal Protestants pass along to their children.

Lest you think that last remark is uninformed prejudice, I should also tell you that my observation of the youthful pilgrims marching through these pages comes alongside my observation of many others in the vast array of religious traditions represented in the United States today. Besides reading the results of recent surveys of youth and young adults,[1] Not long ago I finished writing a book about how American congregations do their work, including passing on a tradition to the children and youth in their midst.[2] With data from 549 congregations, the patterns and contrasts stand out in bold relief.

In sheer organizational energy invested, the contrast between liberal Protestants and everybody else is dramatic. Everybody does some equivalent to children's Sunday school (even Muslims and Buddhists), but mainline Protestants are the only group that routinely does nothing else. Everyone else has weekday programs or day schools or bar mitzvah classes, for instance, but mainline churches are more likely to sponsor a scout troop than to have an organized religious activity for their children (literally). Many mainline kids do not even go to worship services, since children's Sunday school is scheduled at the same time. And in many New England churches, religious education shuts down for the summer. Even a pretty regular attender in many of these churches is lucky to get twenty to thirty hours a year of religious exposure. I can guarantee that these kids will not find biblical words and images creeping into their thoughts twenty years from now!

All of us, looking back on it, found ourselves wondering whether all that Bible reading and memorization was a good thing, but I am now convinced that it is a vital part of forming us. When we commit something to memory, it sinks deep and often resurfaces in surprising ways. As Yvonne Zimmerman puts it, "Whether I like it or not; whether I believe them or not; whether I consciously invoke them or not, these Scriptures have become part of my interaction with my own life." Biblical fragments—knit together in my mother's womb, her price is far above rubies, plans for your welfare and not for harm—happily can also grow with us, providing both a deep touchstone to the past and points of connection to new people and experiences and meaning.

They become, in fact, the common language we speak, part of the tool kit with which we build ourselves and our communities of faith. If nothing else, the Bible's existence means we do not have to start from scratch in building a community. And its infinitely multi-vocal and multi-form self also means that there is plenty of material to work with as we and our communities change.

Listening to this group of pilgrims, I think I have become convinced that having a "canon" matters, not so much because these words are uniquely inspired or holy or true, but because this is the core set of stories we have all agreed to share and that have shaped us and our forebears in manifold ways. There are always other stories and always many interpretations, but those who have called themselves Christian for all these years have these characters and plots in common.

Spending time building up that core is, then, essential. It can later be deconstructed and reconstructed, added to and set aside, but if we do not start here, we may lose something crucial. It is not surprising, of course, that we all look back with such ambivalence about the way we experienced the Bible as children. James Fowler would not be surprised to observe the changes this particular group of young pilgrims has experienced.[3] Looking back, we can see how much we simply trusted our families and our communities to tell us the truth, to tell us stories about what life is like. And looking back it is probably equally predictable that they did not tell us the whole truth. As much as we may feel betrayed when we begin to learn about the Bible's seamier side, that very sense of rupture is a predictable sign of our movement along a developmental path. I often wish that overanxious liberal parents could just relax and tell their children the stories. Never mind that you know all the sinister complications or that you are not entirely sure it is "true." Your six-year-old does not care, and when she does, you will be ready to talk about it.

Indeed, among the striking things about experiences this group of pilgrims recount is that their extended faith community told them the stories *and* provided a place to ask the questions when that time came. Youth groups and classrooms introduced the questions and provoked the debate—within the household of faith. This group of youth did not have to leave the family to explore new territory. Nor were their debates with the tradition a matter of indifference. Unlike fundamentalists—who do a great job of providing the biblical basics but allow inadequte room for debate; and unlike the liberals—who can debate all day but have inadequate basics against which to rebel—this tradition provided the materials for a really good debate and the space in which to have it.

What is also stunning about the experiences recounted here is the way this faith community put its young adults to work. One of the strongest and fastest-growing religions in the world today is the Church of Jesus Christ of Latter-day Saints, and one of the secrets to their success is sending their young adults out on mission. Kids get a challenge and an adventure at a time in life when they want one, but they get that adventure in the company of other Mormons and in the process of trying to convince others to join their movement—something that is very likely to solidify their own commitment to it.

Mennonites do not send kids out door-to-door in black pants and white shirts, but they are no less intent on providing opportunities for young adults to embody the faith. Working for justice in all the ways this group does is no less powerful in solidifying a faith than working to produce converts. Given its grounding in real-world challenges, I suspect that justice work will stand up well as a religious socialization device, well-suited to the challenges of young adulthood and beyond.

It is also fascinating to observe the degree to which these pilgrims are following a path of faith, even as they continue to wrestle with the "truth" of Scripture. They have, in fact, come to a wide range of conclusions on that matter. Chad Martin notes that theirs is a postmodern generation aware of the power to choose, even the power to choose to make something sacred or to give it authority over one's life. I think he's right about that. Once we have seen the wizard, it is hard to take anything at face value again.

Still, this is not a group of nihilists who have given up on Truth. Buffy Garber talks of the freedom she experienced as she began "to realize that some parts of the Bible do not have to be historical facts to be full of truth." Theirs is a recognition that this sort of truth is partly subjective. Tasha Clemmer notes, "It just felt clear that what I experienced as Truth was Truth." But it is also communal. Ryan Beiler talks about how grateful he is to have found "within my church a community of self-described 'evangelical' believers who take the whole of Scripture seriously . . . but also allow for deep questions, ambiguities, and struggles. . . ." As I observe this group of pilgrims, that is a good description of the commitment they share: take the Bible seriously and ask deep questions, recognizing that both of those tasks require your own conscious choice and the support of a community.

Theirs is a commitment that has been nurtured in a remarkable set of institutions. However imperfect, there have been families and churches and schools and places to work that have provided the materials and the skills needed at each step of the way. These are talented, courageous, and committed young adults whose faith is taking many forms and whose current views of Scripture vary widely. But this is also an intrepid band of pilgrims who have been given a great deal of sustenance for their journey. Even today their communities are helping them find ways in which truth can emerge from Scripture to bring comfort and clarity of vision, as well as disturbing questions that demand new answers. I pray that they and their communities may continue to "run and not be weary, to walk and not faint" (Isa. 40:31).

Notes

1. Among the most important recent studies of youth are those coming from the University of North Carolina's "National Study of Youth and Religion,"

such as Christian Smith, "Theorizing Religious Effects Among American Adolescents," *Journal for the Scientific Study of Religion* 42:1 (2003): 17-30. An example of Mainline failures can be found in one of the working papers from the University of Illinois at Chicago's project: R. Stephen Warner, "Two Young United Methodists Speak About Their Religion and Their Parents," available at www.uic.edu/depts/soci/yrp. On the proactive side, the "Way to Live" project at Valparaiso University is developing support for teens in "practicing" the faith, see *"Way to Live: Christian Practices for Teens,"* available from www.waytolive.org. In *Choosing Church: What Makes a Difference for Teens* (Louisville: Westminster John Knox Press, 2004), Carol Lytch has provided an excellent account of how Evangelical, Catholic, and Mainline congregations differ in their work with youth. Accounts of young adult experiences are more scarce, however. The studies reported in *GenX Religion*, Richard W. Flory and Donald E. Miller, eds. (New York: Routledge, 2000) are one exception.

2. Nancy Tatom Ammerman, *Pillars of Faith: American Congregations and Their Partners* (Berkeley: University of California Press, 2004).

3. James Fowler, *Stages of Faith: The Psychology of Human Development and the Quest for Meaning* (Cambridge: Harper & Row, 1981).

CHAPTER 18

Seeing Hope in Deconstruction and Rebuilding

Pam Dintaman

I force myself to go to vespers but feel so dead inside that not even the po-etry of the psalms can penetrate my despair. . . . Then the reading comes; the first words of Genesis, words I read aloud in this church over a month ago, at the Easter Vigil: "In the beginning, God. . . ." I am shocked to re-call how full of life I was that night, shocked to now find myself taken back, against my will, to the garden of creation.
—Kathleen Norris[1]

I post this quote on my wall so I can see it regularly. It speaks of my own journey with Scripture, sometimes finding so much life within the biblical story and other times finding no life. Those dry times feel like "black holes" to me when suddenly the life I previously found in Scrip-ture goes out or dries up. When Norris names this as being "taken back, against my will, to the garden of creation," I can reframe those black holes, those dry spaces, as being a place of new creation. I gain hope that in my despair, *through* my despair, and even through my questions something new may be budding and growing.

Many of the contributors to this volume recall various experiences when they found their faith and beliefs deconstructed in some way. Their faith did not work for them any more in the shape it was in. Jill Landis writes of her faith and beliefs lying in ruins, like a pile of rubble, and speaks to the rebuilding she is experiencing. She tells of the need to come to her own conclusions, not just adhering to conclusions others have previously made. Alicia Miller shares how family crises and relationships with people of other faiths pushed her to examine what shape her own faith and beliefs were in.

These writers' voices speak candidly about what makes sense for their lives and what does not. You can choose to be shocked at the way they speak about Scripture and faith, or you can be amazed that faith and Scripture are taken so seriously that these young men and women believe they must come to a point of honesty to move forward.

Valuing a Broad Spectrum of Voices

A common thread I find in each essay in this collection is the desire to bring many experiences and stories alongside the biblical story. Whether and how the biblical story is relevant to today's issues becomes a primary question. Lee Barrett, my theology professor at Lancaster Theological Seminary (LTS), would remind us that we will never find a perfect denomination. Rather, we should look to see if the church or denomination we are in is struggling, or willing to struggle, with the questions we value as individuals. These new Anabaptists are calling our denomination to listen to the voices on the margin. They refuse to look at the world or at Christianity through only one lens. I believe that desire to listen to different voices both near and far will enrich our faith and our denomination.

As I read, I heard a number of voices give witness to the way the lens of multicultural urban life has changed the way writers view their faith questions. Bethany Spicher Schonberg and Jeremy Garber tell of their increasing awareness of international suffering and poverty in the United States along with military and economic injustices. Jessica King describes how working among and interacting with many different kinds of people moves her to desire "room for us all at the table."

A second lens that changes what these Anabaptists see is an understanding of community that is both global and particular. Kevin Maness suggests "looking for our religion in the meekest of the world's citizens, rather than in the most powerful." Indeed this calls us to recognize that U.S. Mennonite experience has moved from immigrants seeking religious freedom to often being part of the affluent and influential people in communities. Furthermore, Maness mentions Paul's directive to the Philippians that they are to work out their own salvation with fear and trembling. Like those in the early church, we do not do this work alone but neither are the results dictated by the community. The early Anabaptists affirmed the faith community as the locus for interpreting Scripture. Imagine the power of pairing the acknowledgment of our particular lens with a community of diverse experiences and voices in which we interpret Scriptures.

The Willingness to Converse with Scripture and Tradition

Numerous writers mention the faith of their grandparents, even the art on the walls of their homes, and Scripture reading and prayer in the family as significant factors that shaped them as people. By observing the integrity of those early spiritual practices, these young adults feel led to raise questions about these practices; some essayists' grandparents or childhood churches may not accept where they end up as being Anabaptist or even Christian.

By bringing their candor and their own lives to the text, these writers are expressing their hope and belief that God is large enough to hold the questions and doubts. The psalmists model this as they speak their laments and their doubts—"Where are you, God?"—often leading them on toward expressions of praise and gratitude.

When Sunday school teachers focus on producing certain answers, teenagers hear the message that they should leave some of their questions at the church door. The underlying message received is that "Our faith, our God, is not big enough to hold your doubt and questions." King reflects on growing up and having "a great cumulative knowledge of [Bible] trivia" but lacking a biblical understanding that prepared her to step into the complexities of the world. Do teachers and mentors value helping teenagers and young adults move from the "obvious and quantifiable" toward the "nuanced and implied"? Chad Martin recounts how important it was for him to have a pastor who modeled openness to new understanding and growth and being engaged in wrestling with Scripture rather than needing a particular outcome. Jeremy Garber remembers his youth leaders taking his questions seriously and sharing their own passions.

In a class I took with Rabbi Jack Paskoff at LTS, our task was to work our way through Jewish commentaries. He paired us off in the tradition of Judaic Scripture study, challenging us to find the first place in the text where we had a question or an argument. He waited as we sat in a curious, uncomfortable silence reading from the first chapter of Genesis and searching for places of disagreement. As we went further and further into Genesis, he led us back to the first words: "In the beginning. . . ." He asked, "How can there be a beginning if God always was?"

Paskoff told us that one year he may preach on how obedient Abraham was to offer his son Isaac as a sacrifice. The next year, with this same text, he may wonder aloud why Abraham did not argue with God about offering his son Isaac as a sacrifice. Our minds and hearts began to awaken to the invitation to wrestle. As we continued our study, I was amazed at how rabbis from past centuries who took the Scriptures seriously also argued and played with the texts, poked at them, and brought their own experiences and questions to the task of interpreting the stories. Their practice felt unfamiliar to me, making me wonder when it changed for Christians—that there was no more pushing and pulling of the text, its many meanings becoming fewer and set in concrete.

Recently I visited Saint Gregory of Nyssa Episcopal Church in San Francisco, California. I found it refreshing to see members of a Christian congregation state clearly who they hope to be in their community and world—willing to deal with the questions and the complexity of our lives and our contexts. In their "Principles that Guide Us at St. Gregory's," they write, "Our preachers are direct and honest about scholars' questions, skepticism, or doubts about any text—and we preach and share the work of preaching (sermon-sharing) from genuine, living, unresolved personal experience."[2] It is expected that preachers regularly model what it means to wrestle with Scripture.

The Episcopalians at Saint Gregory's declare themselves willing to share with others and be stretched by people of other faith traditions. "We are unashamedly Christian—yet ready to learn from the experience of all people of God."[3] I have been involved in urban Mennonite congregations where this is a practice too, though it has not been stated as an underlying principle.

Within the congregation I serve as pastor, I have begun to recognize new discomfort with a cutting edge. In the past, conformity within a congregation kept differences at a distance; difference was only found between us and the world. Now we are more ready and willing to recognize differences within the congregation, and owning this new reality requires new skills. For example, the diversity within our congregation gives us a place to practice conversing about both common ground and difference. These conversations are untidy and often rigorous.

Martin draws the analogy between his encounters with Scripture and a potter's work with clay: it can be messy. I hear these writers saying they want a church that is not afraid of the messiness. They want Scripture to inform instead of dictate or prescribe their lives. They want to see Scripture as a door, a tool, for meeting God instead of needing to defend Scripture. Malinda Berry describes her delight as a theologian having the permission (and mandate) to ask tough questions of the text. Her call for shared authority brings us back to the early Anabaptists, who wanted Scripture and discernment to rest within the faith community rather than be relegated only to the bishops and clergy. Seeing this wrestling with Scripture as "a journey, not a destination" is a helpful phrase Berry offers us. I wish that for all persons in our congregations—to consider themselves theologians who must bring their own questions to the texts as many founders of the Anabaptist movement did.

Contemporary Anabaptists

Recently I have wondered what defines an Anabaptist today. Are Anabaptist-Mennonites those who believe in the core of *Confession of Faith in a Mennonite Perspective*? Or are contemporary Anabaptists ones who, like the early Anabaptists, question the status quo of their tradition? Conrad Grebel and his peers clearly questioned the church tradition in which they were participating. They asked questions that came from their wrestling with Scripture. Is that questioning part of what makes me an Anabaptist? Or does being an Anabaptist mean I have accepted all the answers formed in the sixteenth century and beyond for the global Mennonite family and other Anabaptist groups? What is our heritage?

From there, I wonder, how do Anabaptists look at Scripture? Does "Scripture alone" guide our theology and ethics, or do we have a broader grid similar to the Methodist Quadrilateral (Scripture, tradition, reason, and experience) mentioned in the introduction and Berry's essay? For the early Anabaptists to take the Protestant Reformation farther than

Martin Luther did, they had to bring their own experience and questions to the mix. Protestant reformers spoke their own questions and took the risk of acknowledging their discomforts with the established church. They had a deep desire to understand Scripture within the context of their world and experience.

I am intrigued and touched by the writers here—whether they claim Christianity currently or believe they have left that framework—who recognize that Scripture surrounds them and influences them in their daily lives, even though the wrestling continues. I, too, grew up in the Mennonite church but learned I was a Mennonite by leaving it. In my years at Church of the Savior, an ecumenical church in Washington, D.C., I learned again what Mennonites are about. Later, I attended a United Church of Christ seminary where high value is placed on ecumenism. There was great openness to learning from the handful of Anabaptist students who were part of the student body. In both settings, people were curious to know more about Anabaptists, and I needed to scramble to find words and to understand how Anabaptist-Mennonites were different from our Christian peers. For this reason I resonate with King's essay as she reflects on her journey to a place of new respect for what Anabaptist-Mennonites can offer the interpretation of Scripture in conversations with people of different beliefs and backgrounds.

Fresh Wind of the Spirit

Verna Dozier writes, "'Behold, I make all things new' is the word of the Lord, but the [church] damns newness as novelty or trend and herds the sheep back to the security of the old fold."[4] She also says, "It is comforting for the church to declare the Bible the Word of God instead of taking seriously what the Bible says—that Jesus himself is the Word of God. It is troubling to consider that God did not become incarnate as a book, but as a person."[5]

Dozier urges us to consider that Jesus continues to nudge us to new understandings of what God desires in our world. But she also realizes that opening ourselves to new understandings often includes facing our fears. "Nothing scares us more than freedom. We are always afraid that freedom will degenerate into chaos—as it often does—so to escape chaos we flee to authority, which means authoritarianism."[6] I find a connection between Dozier's observations and Berry's comment that "I want us all to be allowed to imagine and read out in the open and not be accused of heresy, apostasy, being New Age, or just generally un-Christian."

In the biblical story, a message is continually spoken to the institutional religious bodies: turn around and look with new eyes. Acts 10 and 11 tells of Peter's vision in which the voice of the Lord says, "What God has made clean, you must not call profane" (Acts 10:15). Peter does not limit the meaning of his vision to what food is now acceptable but is able to recognize the vision as a message that God has already embraced people we have considered as unclean or outsiders. Emboldened by this new freedom, Peter welcomes Cornelius, a Roman soldier, and his household into the faith, baptizing them without requiring circumcision.

The biblical story continually shakes our fixed ideas of who God is and what the church is to be about. The early Anabaptists brought their questions and unrest into the established church and shook the doors open. But what about the present? Perhaps we want to think the work is finished and we can be at peace, locking out future questions. But most of us were drawn to, or grew up in, a theology influenced by radical reformers. As heirs of this radical tradition, the contributors to this book and to this ongoing discussion are both looking for and articulating new ways that Scripture guides us but does not close down further discussion and revelation. In their essays, I have found these Anabaptists to have a desire that the church be open to the God who continues to speak to us today through many kinds of texts, our own experiences, and even other cultures and worldviews. We as a church will benefit and thrive by remaining open to the movement of the Spirit today, a spirit that makes all things new, even the Word of God.

Notes

1. Kathleen Norris, *The Cloister Walk* (New York: Putnam Publishing Group, 1995): 239.

2. Saint Gregory of Nyssa Episcopal Church, available from www.saintgregorys.org/Pages/Guiding.html.

3. Ibid.

4. Verna Dozier, *Dream of God: A Call to Return* (Cambridge: Cowley Publications, 1991): 146.

5. Ibid., 89.

6. Ibid., 145.

CHAPTER 19

Reading the
Word and the World

Valerie Weaver-Zercher

Ihad just finished reading the chapters in this book when my mother
was diagnosed with breast cancer. In the weeks that followed, I found
myself simultaneously feeling much older and much younger than I really am: younger because I wanted so badly to pretend that my mom
would live forever, and older because I could no longer do so. Who knew
one could feel both five and fifty?

This sense of both "youthening" and aging was akin to what I felt as
I read the essays in this collection. I became a teenager as I read the writers' accounts of their adolescent years; I lived again the anxiety and exhilaration of my own period of faith questioning. But just as I was getting comfortable in my torn-jeaned, backpack-wielding skin, I would
morph into my fuddy-duddy parental self, asking, "What did these
writers' parents do right in terms of faith development, choice of
church, biblical interpretation, Christian ritual? How can I replicate the
good and avoid the bad with my own kids?"

In addition to this generational leap-frogging, I became aware that
the act of reading these essays constituted much more than simply a
reader (me) reading others' writings. I was re-reading my own journey
with Scripture and Christian faith while I read this text; as Brazilian educator Paulo Freire suggests, my reading of the words in this book implied "continually reading the world," just as "reading the world always
precedes reading the word."[1] Indeed, the writers of these chapters speak

of their readings of both the Word and the world, and their essays testify to the importance of not divorcing the two. Text needs a context; the Word needs the world.

I want to explore three parallel moves that many of the writers—and many of us as readers—make as we re-read our own faith journeys, our views of the Bible, and our understanding of God's role in our lives. These moves are not uniform; the writers do not always move in a straight line from point A to point B. Yet there's just enough harmony between their narratives to embolden me to advance the following readings of their writings.

Reading Our Journeys: From Fracture to Repair

There are countless ways in which this [spiritual journey] may happen: sometimes under conditions which seem to the world like the very frustration of life, of progress, of growth.
—Evelyn Underhill[2]

It is a truism that many Christian young adults undergo a period of doubt as they come to own the faith of their parents. This era is often depicted in one of two ways: either as a predictable stage that will dump the person off exactly where she or he started (and maybe even as a deacon or song-leader), or else as a chosen rebellion brought about by liberal professors and enacted by the piercing of multiple body parts and the imbibing of large quantities of alcohol (or at least returning from Central America "hairy and tanned," as Bethany Spicher Schonberg recounts).

Both representations of this period are fallacious, as the rich stories of these writers tell. My own college-era fracturing of faith was anything but predictable or chosen. I was terrified by the questions that burgled their way into my carefully constructed house of faith, and I tried for a while to bar their entrance. I craved the safety of my high-school understandings of faith and the Bible and longed to be consumed by anything but these unsettling new questions of biblical interpretation, the divinity of Jesus, and the horrific wrongs enacted by the institutional church. And I did none of those wildly unorthodox or sinful things that people who "lose their faith" are supposed to do, to the relieved sighs of my parents even now.

So while stereotyped portrayals of faith crises are often as misleading as they are cliché, the stories contained in this book are not. The metaphors the writers use to describe their crises of faith are telling; they are primarily images of decay. Jill Landis writes, "My theological understandings seemed to crumble to pieces" and Benjamin Beachy describes a "theological breakdown." Alicia Miller recalls, "I kicked at the ashes of my freshly ruined reality," and Daniel Shank Cruz describes "the gradual erosion of my reverence for the Bible." Other writers depict estrangement: Yvonne Zimmerman writes, "Scripture became a stranger to me," while Jessica King imagines her journey with Scripture as an uncomfortably silent car ride with a relative. Whatever image they choose, many of the writers speak of a time of fractured faith, a time when the realities of the world around them could not connect with the Sunday school theologies that had served them well in childhood.

As strong as this collection's faith-fracturing thread, however, is its faith-repairing one. We watch the writers—helped by mentors, classes, spiritual disciplines, and the Bible itself—repair their understandings of Scripture and God and Jesus and the church. Their tools and methods of repair vary: for Jeremy Garber, his return to Christianity "simply made sense"; it also did not hurt that welcoming pastors and a church family nurtured his return trip with conversation and support. For Landis, it was both the story of Nehemiah that enabled her to rebuild her faith as well as a fast from Scripture that provided her with the freshness and energy to return to the text. For Zimmerman, it was the idea that Scripture could inform rather than dictate her life that enabled her to respond with hospitality to the strangeness of the gospel. Conversations with older women about their struggles in the church are what, for Miller, opened up the possibility that she might "cobble together" a faith.

Theirs are not simply refurbished faiths, however, slapped over with a couple coats of paint and glue. While some of the writers have returned to the faith of their parents in most respects, others have ended up with radically different theologies than those into which they were born. For example, Shank Cruz names his current faith "post-Christian." Here lies the unpredictability of the faith journey: the honorable refusal of travelers to confine their destinations to those prescribed by the church, borne out of a commitment to honest truth-seeking. These stories are sure to rankle or even scare church leaders who probably hope for more alignment with Christian credos among their spiritual offspring.

I, however, do not find them frightening. Instead I feel sadness and admiration as I read the stories of those in this group who have not returned to the church in the way that I have. Sadness, because I am connected enough to the church to mourn the leave-taking of such gifted, articulate young adults; admiration, because the honesty with which they approach their journeys is humbling to me, who, at barely thirty, can be complacent and sleepy in the face of questions about faith and the Bible and the church that I used to find invigorating. Thomas Merton challenges contented thirty-somethings like me with these words from *Opening the Bible*: "Let us not be too sure we know the Bible . . . just because we have learned not to have problems with it." He continues, "Have we ceased to question the book and be questioned by it?"[3]

Merton's image of the Bible as a conversation partner leads to the next move that occurs for many of these writers: from viewing the Bible as a tract to viewing it as a poem.

Reading the Bible: From Tract to Poem

Texts cannot create meaning, just as hammers cannot build houses.
Humans create meaning with texts and from texts.
—Jeff Deroshia[4]

In this collection of essays and stories, many of the young adults speak of their movement from viewing the Bible as a lesson plan designed to convert wrong action into right (a tract) to viewing the Bible as a much more wild, unruly collection of writings (a poem).

For help in understanding this, I turn to literary theorist Louise Rosenblatt, who articulated the reader-response theory of reading (also called transactional theory) that attempts to explain how readers make meaning out of words. Rosenblatt's theory centers on the idea that meaning inheres not in the words of a text itself but in the *interaction* between the text and the reader.[5] Reader-response theory suggests that, as teacher-educator R. E. Probst explains, "the relationship between the reader and text is much like that between the river and its banks, each working its effect upon the other, each contributing to the shape of the poem."[6] Rosenblatt developed her theory in the wake of formalist or New Critical ideas, which claimed that texts contain a single, unassailable Meaning, and that the job of the reader is to figure It out. Reader-response theory ousts the text as sole determiner of Meaning and forces it to share authority with the reader, who brings all of her or his experiences, opinions, and emotions to bear on the text.

The faith journeys of many writers in this anthology echo this move from formalism to transactionality, from a belief that meaning is held *within* texts to a belief that meaning is created *between* the text and reader. Listen to their voices: Garber observes, "A story without a reader lies on the page like lifeless mud in the Garden of Eden"; Maness states, "Much of [the Bible] has meaning for me only if I create that meaning in the act of reading it"; and Martin simply says, "If the Bible is to be considered sacred, I must choose to make it sacred."

In general, these writers prefer to converse with the Bible rather than submit to it. This might seem wrong-headed at best and blasphemous at worst. Yet in the framework of transactional theory, these writers are just being honest about the process in which all readers engage: using our experiences and memories to create meaning.

Certainly the meaning of most texts, including the Bible, is more stable than the meaning of my three-year-old son's scrawls, which, according to him, one moment read, "Dear Mr. Ron, How are you?" and the next moment mean, "This is a picture of a mountain." There are connections between the signifier and the signified, between "what the Bible really says" and how you and I understand it, between the words and the Word. But reader-response theory helps us understand how it is possible for my uncle to read the Scripture and claim that Jesus died to pacify a vengeful God and for me to read the same text and believe that Jesus died to absorb the violence of the world in a way that shows us how to do the same.

Rosenblatt also claims that, in addition to our preconceptions and histories and social standing, the stance we take when we read a text is crucial to determining our interpretation. *Efferent* reading means looking at a text for information or guidance in a task; the term comes from the Latin root *effere*, "to carry away." I read efferently when I page through my computer manual or skim the day's headlines, or when I thumb through the pages of my Bible to find the best verse to support my opinion about women in leadership or homosexuality. It is certainly a bonus if the prose of a computer manual or newspaper or Bible contains lovely rhythm and metaphor and images, but when I am reading efferently, such aesthetic fulfillment is an add-on, not a requirement.

Efferent reading is the stance that many of the young adults in this collection remember being taught as children: Zimmerman's index cards for memorizing Bible verses, Spicher Schonberg's summer "proverb-and-chore-lists," Maness's early sense that every story in the Bible taught some element of "right living." And although the resulting actions were quite different, it is also the stance that many of the writers struck as teenaged or college-aged readers, looking for answers to those bothersome Bible questions like whether hell exists, whether Jesus is the only way to God, and whether Scripture is innately oppressive for women. As Malinda Berry writes of the stance she struck in college, "The Bible functioned as a tool—nothing less, nothing more." In actuality, efferent reading asks little of the text, requiring nothing in the way of pleasure or poetry or even likeability. Just give me a sound byte with which to convince my uncle or a moral that will keep my kids in line.

Aesthetic reading, on the other hand, looks not to carry away information but to *experience* the text in its full aesthetic, intellectual, or emotional intensity. Aesthetic reading is less directive and less focused on outcomes than an efferent stance; it requires that the reader be fully present as she or he reads the text, and that she or he be cognizant of the memories, associations, and fleeting thoughts that the text births. An aesthetic stance values rhythm and sensation more than lesson and dictum.

Judging from the essays in this collection, encounters with Scripture which prove to be the most transformative grow out of aesthetic as opposed to efferent experiences with the Bible: Spicher Schonberg's tears and desire to shout out of her window upon reading a verse from 1 Corinthians; Martin's delight in slides of ancient clay pots in a seminary class, which encouraged him to "fearlessly play in the mud and . . . not worry about the fire"; Zimmerman's befriending of Scriptures and their "beauty, their wildness, their terror, their power." Sometimes an aesthetic reading even coexists with and then overtakes an efferent one. Garber mentions the comfort he found in a particular verse, even though it was "certainly out of context in its application to me."

Perhaps this should not be surprising, considering that aesthetic reading is the lesser taught and therefore the less stale of the two stances. From early on, most of us were schooled to read efferently. In Sunday school we were asked, "What does the Bible tell us to do?" or "What's the lesson that Jesus taught us?" In school, it was just a slight permutation: "What's the main idea of this story?" or "Read the next paragraph and answer questions one through twelve." Aesthetic reading was for Judy Blume books on the bus ride home or some Shel Silverstein poems on the weekends. Essayist Sarah Kehrberg was fortunate enough to grow up in a home where Bible stories nestled comfortably beside other imagination-capturing tales like Narnia and Peter Pan; it was in Sunday school, she writes, "where *concepts* were taught" (emph. mine). According to literary critic Alan Purves, Kehrberg's early aesthetic experiences with the Bible are rare; he claims that "a large portion of the American population does not or cannot read most texts aesthetically," and that society tends to "depoeticize" texts by pushing the efferent mode upon its readers.[7]

This reality raises numerous questions for us as readers of the Bible, and I also hear these questions with the ears of a parent. How can we teach aesthetic reading of Scripture to our children? How do we stop viewing the aesthetic stance toward any text, especially the Bible, as inferior to the efferent one? How do we stop depoeticizing the text and begin to simply "play around in the mud"?[8]

I do not want to imply that efferent readings of Scripture are useless. As high school and college students enter new stages of intellectual rigor, an efferent stance toward Scripture sharpens and clarifies their relationship to God and the world. An efferent stance is not the same as a literalistic one, and it is far from wrong to think that we can carry away lessons and inspiration and challenge from the Bible. Rather, the efferent mode is harmful only to the extent to which it dwarfs the aesthetic.

Reader-response theory, while a helpful lens through which to read these chapters, verges on individualism and ahistoricism in its focus on the *individual* reader in the *particular* reading moment. While it stresses the context of the reader, which might include her or his community, reader-response theory deemphasizes the profound role of a gathered community in the interpretive event. Several writers in this collection offer helpful correctives to Rosenblatt's theory by "Anabaptizing" it— that is, introducing the crucial elements of *community* and *history*. King writes of how empty her journey with Scripture would be without the "counsel and relationship of other believers who want to journey together." Beiler echoes that sense of the value of "community and honest dialogue in one's approach to the Bible." Zimmerman stresses that insofar as the Bible has been part of Anabaptist Christians' "web of meaning" for centuries, "we are well advised to be hospitable to the ways of making meaning that have served us throughout time—not because these things must continue to serve us in the same ways, but because they have been our friends and teachers."

Even while this volume offers the beginnings of an Anabaptist theory of reading, however, the similarities between the writers' contexts limits its scope. For while the writers in this collection repeatedly emphasize the particularity of the biblical writers and their cultures, fewer of them articulate how their own particularities of background and culture and time influence their *readings* of Scripture. Every reading event, and every reading life for that matter, hangs in a thick shroud of intentions and backgrounds and memories of the specific reader. In many ways, that is what this volume is about: making visible, through stories, the contextual clouds that swathe Anabaptist-related young adults in the first part of the twenty-first century. By expressing this theme, this book takes seriously the foundational idea of a transactional theory of reading: the context of the reader determines the meaning of the text.

To probe even deeper I ask the following questions. If a reader's context is so determinative of textual meaning, what difference does it make that all of this collection's writers are college-educated? For the most part socio-economically privileged? North American? And, as the editors consciously chose, Anabaptist-related? Is there a way to be honest about the ways in which our social statuses, chosen or ascribed, influence our readings of Scripture?

And is there a way to now set these voices in conversation with other voices, such as those of the "younger evangelicals" about whom sociologist Robert Webber writes in his book, *The Younger Evangelicals: Facing the Challenges of the New World?*[9] The twenty-something believers in Webber's study are more literal in their understandings of Scripture and more convinced of traditional faith doctrines than many of the contributors to this volume. Webber and others, including Dan Kimball who writes of a youthful turn to "vintage Christianity" in his recent book *The Emerging Church*, see many young Christians veering toward a creedal, evangelistic faith.[10] How can these "younger evangelicals" and "younger Anabaptists" talk with each other? If I view the Bible primarily as a poem, how can I talk with those who view it as a tract, without their viewing me as heretical, without *my* viewing *them* as close-minded?

Reading God's Role: From Pursued to Pursuer

It was not I that found, O Savior true, no, I was found of thee.
—excerpt from hymn text "I Sought the Lord"[11]

Several of the young adults in this collection speak of near-obsessive practices of spiritual disciplines in childhood and adolescence: Zimmerman's index cards of memory verses, Spicher Schonberg's morning devotions, and Buffy Garber's read-throughs of her lavender Precious Moments Bible. I, too, did the whole routine, probably before I turned twelve: reading the Bible the whole way through, putting tracts in phone booths as an assignment for my pre-baptism class, fearfully contemplating the verse about the unpardonable sin, keeping a list of "prayer requests" and "prayers answered"—even getting up after I had gone to bed to jot down just one more, then one more.[12]

Present in many of these narratives is an adolescent pursuit of God through the venues we were being taught in church: reading and memorizing the Bible, sharing our faith, obeying authority. I doubt our pastors knew how compulsive and guilt-ridden we were becoming, and no doubt, some would have applauded our sincere and rather endearing efforts. Some, however, had they known how we were translating their sermons into spiritual self-flagellation, would have helped us find more age-appropriate ways of experiencing a God who pursues us.

I appreciate Zimmerman's challenge to extend "hospitality to these parts of who we have been," to these childish and adolescent forms of faith. I do not want to denigrate my early spiritual disciplines for their vapidity or rigidity; indeed, the paradox here is that those mostly guilt-induced daily devotions are what enable several writers—and myself—to at times feel "pursued" by God through Scripture. As she writes, her rigidly memorized verses "still routinely spring to mind; they move within me; they poke their heads like freshly sprouted plants in spring." Tasha Clemmer writes of her sense that "the text has returned" to her, and Krista Dutt writes that the Bible "continues to make unexpected moves." Many of them write with gratitude for the meaning and comfort familiar passages bring. How can one be pursued by Scripture that one does not know? How can a text return if it's never been there in the first place? How can the Bible make unexpected moves if one hasn't somehow learned what to expect?

Yet as a mother, I crave direction in helping my children find authentic, age-appropriate ways to approach God without guilt or compulsion. I wonder how to help children feel lovingly and longingly pursued by God rather than beating themselves up for not following God frequently or earnestly enough. As an Anabaptist, I believe that there will be time enough for individual spiritual disciplines when children are old enough to truly choose to practice them for themselves. Meanwhile, I wonder how to help them become familiar enough with Scripture so that it returns to them with new meaning as they grow—yet not over-saturate them with it.[13]

I also realize that I cannot control all of my children's experiences with Scripture; in fact, I am sure that through Sunday school and friends and summer camp, they will learn permutations of the Christian faith that make me wince. My own parents certainly never told me that I needed to read through the Bible when I was eleven; my overactive conscience simply translated what I heard at church into a mandate for my own life. Yet I also am not ready to keep my kids out of church until I screen all their Sunday school teachers to make sure their theologies line up with my own.

So I end here as my conventional old parent self, trying to imagine what my children might write in a similar book twenty years from now. I hope their chapters will be as honest, as concerned about people on the margins, and as faithful to their understandings of God as the writings in this collection. I pray that my children will tell, like these writers have, of the ways that faith must sometimes be broken before it can grow, of how the Bible can make you cry, and of a God who pursues us with a love that makes all our pursuits look feeble indeed.

Notes

1. Paulo Freire, "The Importance of the Act of Reading," in *Literacy: Reading the Word and the World,* Paulo Freire and Donaldo Macedo (New York: Bergin & Garvey, 1987): 25.

2. Evelyn Underhill, *The Spiritual Life* (New York: Harper & Brothers, 1937): 32.

3. Thomas Merton, *Opening the Bible* (Collegeville, Minn.: The Liturgical Press, 1970): 27.

4. Jeff Deroshia, "Construction and Construal: An Analysis of the Architec

ture and Assembly of Reading," *Split Shot: A Journal of Writing* 1:2 (www.wow-schools.net/Split_Shot/archive/volume1/issue2/comment/construction.html).

5. See Louise Rosenblatt, *The Reader, the Text, the Poem: The Transactional Theory of the Literary Work* (Carbondale, Ill: Southern Illinois University Press, 1979).

6. R. E. Probst, "Transactional Theory in the Teaching of Literature," ERIC Clearinghouse on Reading and Communication Skills (Urbana, 1987): ED284274. The "poem," for Rosenblatt, was not any poem on the page, but the meaning created between the text and the reader.

7. See Alan Purves, "The Aesthetic Mind of Louise Rosenblatt," *Reader* 20 (1988): 68-77.

8. Catholic educator Sofia Cavalletti's work on the "parable method" of reading Scripture with children provides a partial answer to these questions. She claims that the characteristics of childhood—wonder, metaphoric thinking, love, joy, and a sense of communion—make children uniquely able to approach Scripture aesthetically. Catherine Maresca, director of the Center for Children and Theology, offers ideas for reading parables with children based on Cavelletti's ideas: communal meditation on the parable that includes savoring its images, manipulation of materials that allows the children to further reflect on and illustrate the parable, the careful selection of questions that help children experience the text rather than those which "test" the children's understanding of it. An aesthetic stance before the text "allows the children to enjoy the revelations of the parable, and further, to create a meeting place with God therein," Maresca writes. See Catherine Maresca, "Poems and Parables," *Occasional Papers* 1, 1 (Center for Children and Theology, January 2000): 8-9.

9. See Robert Webber, *The Younger Evangelicals: Facing the Challenges of the New World* (Grand Rapids: Baker Book House, 2002).

10. See Dan Kimball, Rick Warren, Brian D. McLaren, *The Emerging Church* (Grand Rapids: Zondervan, 2003).

11. *Hymnal: A Worship Book* (Scottdale, Pa.: Mennonite Publishing House, 1992): 506.

12. Interestingly enough—and rather too interesting to explore in-depth here—is the fact that most of the anecdotes of compulsive childhood devotional practices come from the women in the collection. What was it about being "good little Christian girls" in the 1970s and 1980s that made us feel guilty for not spending at least a half-hour "with God" every day?

13. See Sara Wenger Shenk, *Anabaptist Ways of Knowing: A Conversation about Tradition-Based Critical Education* (Telford, Pa.: Cascadia Publishing House, 2003), in which she moderates a conversation among several scholars about the traditions and rituals of faith communities that nurture and educate children.

Eating the Ancient, Brittle, Bitter Scroll: A Reading

Krista Dutt

Four readers needed, with the fourth needing to be a woman. This is a circle of four people talking with each other in some sense—but also participating in a liturgical reading with whatever connotation that phrase may bring. Each time a Bible passage is read, the person reading it needs to take a step forward to give it more emphasis. The four people need to see the struggle and be able to express it, but at the same time not get too wrapped up in the struggle because they are still committed to eating the scroll. However, because the dialogue does not give answers to these hard passages, participants and the gathered group will be left with tension rather than resolution.

Reader #1: *(To readers and congregation)* Have you ever thought that the Bible was just too complex to understand? I find the Bible inspiring, yet quite troubling. For instance, how should I react to David?

Reader #2: *(Take step out to place emphasis)* David rose from his couch and was walking about on the roof of the king's house, when he saw from the roof a woman bathing; the woman was quite beautiful. . . . David sent messengers to get her, and she came to him, and he lay with her (2 Sam. 11:2, 4). In a letter David wrote, "Set Uriah in the forefront of the hardest fighting, then draw back from him, so that he may be struck down and die" (2 Sam. 11:15).

Reader #1: *(Confident)* I do realize that David was a good person over-all. *(A big however)* However, an anointed king who commits adultery and then kills a righteous man to hide the truth? Not exactly how I see God working. God illuminates the truth—God doesn't hide it. Am I missing something?

Reader #3: But a perfect God has no perfect people to deal with. . . .

Reader #2: *(Directly to Reader #3)* But isn't the purpose of the Scriptures to lead us to the way to be?

Reader #3: *(Not solving the problem, but questioning as Reader #2)* But David ends up showing me how not to do something—isn't that a lesson of truth?—even if it is unusual means? Anyway, those aren't the types of passages that bother me. *(Noticeably troubled)* The Scripture that bothers me is in Acts.

Reader #4: *(Take step out to place emphasis)* All who believed were to-gether and had all things in common; they would sell their posses-sions and goods and distribute the proceeds to all, as any had need. Day by day, as they spent much time together in the temple, they broke bread at home and ate their food with glad and gener-ous hearts, praising God and having the goodwill of all the people (Acts 2:44-47a).

Reader #3: What is that all about? How in today's society am I to carry this out? Any ideas?

Reader #1: Join Mennonite Voluntary Service?

Reader #2: Take a black Sharpie marker and cross it out. Ignore it!

Reader #4: Believe it as what heaven is, rather than what earth should be?

Reader #3: That is the problem: even if I would want to do this we couldn't agree on how to do it. Plus, living in North America, I won't be able to live as simply as, say, a person from Africa, which makes it all the more confusing.

Reader #2: You know what else is confusing—Jesus' teachings! What about. . . .

Reader #1: *(Take step out to place emphasis)* You have heard that it was said, "You shall love your neighbor and hate your enemy." But I say to you, Love your enemies and pray for those who persecute you. . . (Matt. 5:43).

Reader #2: *(With chip on shoulder)* Yeah, this works in theory; it sounds good, especially for telling little children, or people who see us as their enemies, or for those who are in oppression, but I can't use it in practice. Exactly what is the definition of love?

Reader #4: Love—not hate.

Reader #1: Love—not liking what the person's actions are all the time, but trying to understand why they think and act the way they do.

Reader #3: Love—a way of being; not vengeful, not ignoring, and allowing others to be empowered.

Reader #2: *(Truthful)* The only thing that keeps me from ignoring this passage is that Jesus had plenty of enemies and he seemed to love them. But the truth is—following Jesus is hard!

Reader #4: I appreciate what the Bible is and does for me in my daily life. But what I can't figure out is the whole issue of contradictory statements in the Bible. For example. . . .

Reader #3: *(Take step out to place emphasis)* Let a woman learn in silence with full submission. I permit no woman to teach or to have authority over a man; she is to keep silent. For Adam was formed first, then Eve; and Adam was not deceived, but the woman was deceived and became a transgressor. Yet she will be saved through childbearing, provided they continue in faith and love and holiness, with modesty (1 Tim. 2:11-15).

Reader #4: How can I be a child of God, which Genesis says, and be asked at the same time to be silent about my Creator? Why can Esther be a leader of her people, yet women are asked to be silent after the church starts? Why is this wonderful book so wishy-washy sometimes?

Reader #2: It holds different streams of thought?

Reader #3: It tells stories to illustrate the truth, which are bound to disagree?

Reader #4: I know the Bible is a book of possibility—each of us can probably find something to relate to, but that doesn't make trying to figure out the meaning any easier, in fact (*confirming what Reader #2 said, looking at him or her*), it *is* downright hard.

Reader #1: But, no matter how hard it is, I still want to study this book.

Reader #2: I still want to try to understand this Scripture.

Reader #3: I still want to identify myself with these words.

Reader #4: I still want to grow within its pages.

Subject Index

Scripture Index

The Contributors

Nancy Tatom Ammerman is professor of Sociology of Religion at Boston University and an active member of First Baptist Church in Newton, Massachusetts. She grew up in Missouri, Arizona, and California and graduated from Southwest Baptist College in Bolivar, Missouri (where she met her husband, Jack Ammerman). She went from there to the University of Louisville and then to Yale University, where she earned her Ph.D. She has written widely on conservative religious movements and on American congregational life. Her most recent book is *Pillars of Faith: American Congregations and Their Partners* (University of California Press).

Benjamin Beachy is a graduate student and the Application Development Manager at Eastern Mennonite University (EMU). He completed his B.S. at EMU and spent a year in Mennonite Voluntary Service in La Jara, Colorado. Benjamin is an active member of Lindale Mennonite Church in Linville, Virginia, and is married to Sarah Diener Beachy.

Ryan Beiler lives in Washington, D.C., where he has been the Web Editor for *Sojourners* magazine since 1999. He grew up at Spruce Lake Retreat and Wilderness Camp in the Pocono Mountains of Pennsylvania and is a graduate of Lancaster Mennonite High School and Ithaca College with a degree in Cinema and Photography (with minors in English, Spanish, and Religious Studies). Ryan is a member of Washington Community Fellowship and serves on its Damascus Road Racial Justice Team and as president of the board of Urban Family Development, the church's local neighborhood ministry.

Malinda Elizabeth Berry is a graduate of both Goshen College, where she received a double B.A. in History and English, and of Associated Mennonite Biblical Seminary, where she completed a M.A. in Peace Studies. She is currently working and teaching at Goshen College as Visiting Scholar in Religion and Women's Studies while she completes her doctoral degree in Systematic Theology from Union Seminary in the City of New York. She is a member of Berkey Avenue Mennonite Fellowship.

Tasha Clemmer, originally from Lancaster, Pennsylvania, lives in New York City, where she teaches high school math at a public high school in Manhattan. She received her M.A. in Secondary Math Education in June 2006 from The City College of New York. In her free time she enjoys biking, reading, snowboarding, whitewater kayaking, and gardening.

Pam Dintaman serves as pastor at Community Mennonite Church of Lancaster in Lancaster, Pennsylvania. She previously was a pastor at Southside Fellowship in Elkhart, Indiana, and worked as director of Deaf Ministries for Mennonite Board of Missions. She is married to Larry Gingrich and they have two young adult children, Kelsey and Carly.

Krista Dutt, originally from central Ohio, resides in Chicago, Illinois. She directs DOOR Chicago, an urban education program which partners with Mennonite Mission Network and Presbyterian Church USA. In her free time, she enjoys cooking, karaoke, and exploring Chicago. She is a member of First Church of the Brethren in Chicago.

Buffy Garber received her B.A. in Early Childhood and Elementary Education from Goshen College and has taken classes at Associated Mennonite Biblical Seminary in Elkhart, Indiana. Now residing in Denver, Colorado, with her husband Jeremy and daughter Fiona, she attends First Universalist Church and is an advocate for attachment parenting and extended breast-feeding.

Jeremy Garber graduated from Goshen College with a B.A. in Theatre and from Associated Mennonite Biblical Seminary with an M.Div. in Theology and Ethics. He is currently enrolled in the joint doctoral program in Theology, Philosophy, and Cultural Studies at the Iliff School of Theology and University of Denver. His proposed dissertation topic is a Mennonite theology of popular culture. Jeremy, his wife Buffy, and daughter Fiona currently attend First Universalist Church in Denver, Colorado, where Jeremy leads the Unitarian Universalist Christian Fellowship.

Keith Graber Miller is professor of Bible, Religion, and Philosophy at Goshen College, specializing in ethics and theology. He is author of *Wise as Serpents, Innocent as Doves: American Mennonites Engage Washington* (University of Tennessee Press, 1996), editor of *Teaching to Transform: Perspectives on Mennonite Higher Education* (Pinchpenny Press, 2001), and writer of a dozen chapters for other edited texts. He completed his Ph.D. at Emory University, his M.Div. at Associated Mennonite Biblical Seminary, and his B.A. at Franklin College. Keith is an ordained minister in Mennonite Church USA and an active member of Assembly Mennonite Church in Goshen, Indiana. He is the husband of Ann Graber Miller and father of three children—Niles, Mia, and Simon.

Sarah Kehrberg graduated from Bethel College, North Newton, Kansas, with degrees in Music and History. She worked for four years at Mennonite Publishing Network as an editor. She currently homemakes in Lexington, Kentucky with her husband and two young daughters. She attends Oasis Community Church.

Jessica King grew up in Lancaster County, Pennsylvania, and now lives in Pittsburgh, Pennsylvania, where she is the Executive Director of the Union Project—an effort to transform a formerly abandoned church into an arts and enterprise incubator. She was formerly the Executive Director of Mennonite Urban Corps and has served on several boards and committees of local community development corporations. She attends East Liberty Presbyterian Church and Stone Soup, a Mennonite small group.

Jill Landis, a native of Indiana, graduated from Eastern Mennonite University with a degree in Philosophy and Religion. She has served in volunteer assignments in the United States and overseas, has worked for several Mennonite organizations/institutions, and is a free lance writer. A member of Park View Mennonite Church, Harrisonburg, Virginia, she loves learning new and profound things from the kids she teaches.

Kevin Maness lived in New York City for three years while studying for a Ph.D. at New York University. While in New York City, he lived in Menno House and became a member of Manhattan Mennonite Fellowship. Kevin now lives in Pennsylvania, where he teaches at Eastern University. He is a member of Radnor Monthly Meeting (Society of Friends).

Chad Martin lives in Pittsburgh, Pennsylvania, with his wife Jessica King, daughter Esmé, and Labrador retriever Sadie. In 2006—having crafted a thesis on theology, creativity and art-making—he received an M.A. in theology from Pittsburgh Theological Seminary. He is also a stay-at-home dad, potter, and art teacher. His B.A. in Studio Arts is from Goshen College. He also helped found Stone Soup, a Mennonite-related house church in which he still participates, and he attends East Liberty Presbyterian Church.

Alicia Miller, now living in New York City, is originally from Indianapolis, Indiana. After finishing her degree at City University of New York School of Law in summer 2007, Alicia looks forward to beginning her career in international human rights law. She currently does not attend church but finds great renewal, accountability, and inspiration in the world of human rights work, in all of its various incarnations.

Daniel Shank Cruz, originally from New York City and Lancaster, Pennsylvania, currently lives in DeKalb, Illinois, where he is pursuing a Ph.D. in British and American Literature at Northern Illinois University. He is a graduate of Goshen College and has published articles in various Mennonite publications and edited *How Julia Kasdorf Changed My Life: Reflections on Mennonite Identity* (Pinchpenny Press, 2001). His current research interests include LGBT (lesbian, gay, bisexual, transgender) literature and the relationships between literature and movements for social change.

Bethany Spicher Schonberg lived most recently in Washington, D.C., where she worked as a legislative assistant at the Mennonite Central Committee Washington Office and attended Community House Church. She studied International Agriculture at Eastern Mennonite University, and in 2006 she and her spouse Micah made a six-month, cross-country tour of sustainable farms.

Valerie Weaver-Zercher is a free lance writer and editor and full-time mother. She has taught writing and literacy in various capacities, most recently in southeastern Kentucky under the auspices of Mennonite Central Committee. Having graduated from Eastern Mennonite University with a B.A. in English in 1994, she served as assistant editor of *Gospel Herald*, the former magazine of the Mennonite Church. In 2000 she completed an M.A. in Reading/Writing/Literacy from the University of Pennsylvania. Valerie and her husband David and three young sons live in Grantham, Pennsylvania.

Yvonne C. Zimmerman is a Ph.D. candidate in the Religion and Social Change concentration of the joint Ph.D. program in Religious and Theological Studies at Iliff School of Theology and University of Denver, in Denver, Colorado. During the 2005-06 year she was a predoctoral fellow at the Fisher Center for the Study of Women and Men, Hobart and William Smith Colleges in Geneva, New York. She completed her Master of Theological Studies degree at Emory University's Candler School of Theology and her B.A. at Goshen College.

Printed in the United States
65242LVS00006B/199-210

9 781931 038379